WAR AND PEACE IN THE WORLD'S RELIGIONS

WAR AND PEACE
IN THE WORLD'S RELIGIONS

JOHN FERGUSON

NEW YORK

OXFORD UNIVERSITY PRESS

1978

Library of Congress Cataloging in Publication Data

Ferguson, John, 1921-
    War and peace in the world's religions.

    Includes bibliographies and index.
    1. War and religion.   2.   Peace (Theology)
I.   Title.
BL65.W2F47   1978   291.1'7873   78-19191
ISBN 0-19-520073-X
ISBN 0-19-520074-8 pbk.

For
Hilary and
Dick

The Author

Professor John Ferguson is Dean and Director of Studies in Arts at The Open University. After taking a classics degree with first class honours at St John's College, Cambridge, he taught classics in the universities of Durham and London and held professorships in classics at Ibadan and Minnesota Universities. He has held visiting professorships at Hampton Institute, and the universities of Nigeria and Florida. He is much involved with the Christian Peace Movement and is the joint editor of Reconciliation Quarterly. *He is a member of numerous academic and voluntary organizations and the author of many plays and books. His many recreations include cricket, drama, opera and madrigals.*

CONTENTS

Throughout this book dates have been designated C.E. (Christian or Common Era) in place of A.D. which the author considers inappropriate when referring to non-Christian religions.

ACKNOWLEDGEMENTS

Biblical quotations from the Revised Standard Version of the Bible, copyright 1946, 1952, © 1971 by the Division of Christian Education of the National Council of the Churches of Christ in the United States of America, are used by permission.

Extracts from the New English Bible, © 1961, 1970, are used by permission of the Delegates of the Oxford University Press and the Syndics of the Cambridge University Press.

PREFACE

I have greatly welcomed the opportunity to write this book, and am grateful to Professor Parrinder and to Sheldon Press for the invitation. Curiously enough, though a lot has been written about war and peace in relation to Christianity, and a certain amount in relation to Judaism, I have not really come across very much explicitly on the subject in relation to other religions, and have had to draw on my own reading of primary sources and to elicit the relevant material from broader surveys. For this reason it has been a relief to find writings of more direct relevance. I was happy to come on M. Khadduri *War and Peace in the Law of Islam*, an authoritative study. For Judaism I gladly acknowledge my indebtedness to Rabbi Hirsch's really excellent booklet *Thy Most Precious Gift: Peace in Jewish Tradition*, which taught me much, and which I have consequently shamelessly pillaged. Similarly for Buddhism I have drawn freely and closely on Dr Saddhatissa's *Buddhist Ethics*. I am grateful also to Professor Trevor Ling for allowing me to draw on a presently unpublished paper on 'Buddhism and Aggression, National and Personal'. But my particular debts are discernible in the bibliographies to each chapter.

When I was first a university teacher it was expected that I would pretend not to believe in anything. More recently students have demanded that we reveal our presuppositions so that they may be discounted. This is a healthier state of affairs. I do not pretend to be uncommitted. I am myself a Christian and a pacifist, and a pacifist because a Christian. But I also believe that Christ calls us to love and respect and be open towards those of other faiths. I have learned much from them, as I have learned also from non-pacifists. I hope my own commitment has not twisted my presentation. This is not a book of advocacy, but an attempt at understanding. I owe a great debt to successive secretaries, Lynne Fryer, Susan Darling and Karen Smith, who have coped splendidly with a difficult manuscript, and to my wife for another admirable index.

JOHN FERGUSON

Chapter 1

TRIBAL RELIGION

THE NATURE OF TRIBAL RELIGION

Tribal religion is not easy to define. It has sometimes been called 'primitive religion', but the word 'primitive' has a pejorative tone and is inappropriate to, for example, a sophisticated civilization such as that of the West African Yoruba. John Taylor called his well-known book *Primal Religion*. That is better, for it indicates that we may see religion stripped of some of the accretions which have emerged during the more rapid and far-reaching economic, social and historical changes which have swept Europe in recent centuries. Yet in the strict sense primal religion applies to the families of the Dordogne caves, the burial customs discernible in isolated finds from remote pre-history, the fertility figurines of Willendorf or Lespugues. Equally, the phrase 'tribal religion' may be criticized, for the religious customs and attitudes we shall here examine sometimes extend beyond the boundaries of a single tribe.

Religion is seen as an aspect or dimension of the whole of life. There is no distinction between the secular and the sacred. All that we do we do under divine powers.

Religion is social, communal. The basic unit is the family. But the family is a part of the tribe, and a family which neglects its religious observances is not a law to itself, but may endanger the whole tribe. Religion is thus political. Its sphere is everything that concerns the life of the community; its most prominent concerns are those which are most prominent in the life of the community – birth and death, food, health, security, counsel. War and peace are among these.

Tribal religion is not generally monotheistic. This assertion is assailable and needs some qualification, and certainly tribal religion may bear the seeds of monotheism. Many tribes have a Most-High god, for example, Olodumare among the Yoruba, Zeus in ancient Greek religion, Wotan among the Scandinavians. Other gods are his ministers; he is the king, they the barons – or rather they are all kings and he the king of kings. Or again tribal religion is sometimes henotheistic: the tribe has its own god, as Chemosh was god of the Moabites, while not denying the existence of the gods of other tribes. But there is a general tendency to believe in a multiplicity of divine powers, each with its own sphere of influence. This often means a god of war, and sometimes a god or goddess of peace.

Different tribes have different religious systems. Expansion and conquest may sometimes mean that conquered peoples adopt the gods of their conquerors. Sometimes also there is assimilation: a people as it expands encounters unfamiliar gods, and may take them into its own pantheon or identify them with its own deities; the Romans were adept at this last. Graeco-Roman religion was tribal in origin, but took on some of the characteristics of a universal or world religion.

Fundamentally, religion involves acceptance. Nonconformity, free thinking, atheism and the like are found only when the social bonds have weakened. Religion itself is what is, rather than what ought to be.

The aim of religion is to be right with the divine powers, to attain what the ancient Romans called the *pax deorum*, the favour of the gods.

THE RELIGION OF THE ANCIENT GREEKS

The Hellenes who invaded Greece from the north in the second millennium B.C. brought with them the great Indo-European sky-god, Dyaus, or Zeus. It has been said that this is all we know about them. With him came a shadowy consort, Dione, and a Valkyrie-like figure, Pallas, the Maiden, a warrior-goddess. They encountered the mother-goddess in various forms: Dione dropped out of the picture, and Zeus acquired as his consort Hera ('our Lady'), the mother-goddess of Argos. Pallas became identified with the pre-Hellenic goddess of Athens as Pallas Athene.

The poems attributed to Homer show a fully-fledged pantheon with differentiation of function. Zeus is the overlord, the commander-in-chief, the father of gods and men. He presides over the Council of the Twelve Olympians; the domestic deity, Hestia, power of the hearth, was later pushed out by Dionysus, a power of wild nature, ecstasy and intoxication. But there were all along other supernatural beings, like Pan, the spirit of the wildwood, and the nymphs who animated springs and trees, river-gods and the like.

The god whose special function was war was named Ares. The etymology of the name is quite unknown. Although mythologically he was son of Zeus and Hera, it does not seem likely that he was a Greek god in origin. He seems to have been a Thracian god in fact; he has been supposed a sun-god, but he was more probably just a war-god there as in Greece. He is found siding with enemies of the Greeks, Trojans and Amazons. He is called 'hateful', 'man-murdering'. Zeus actually says to him:

You are the most hateful to me of all the gods who inhabit Olympus, loving strife, wars and battles as you always do.

Homer *Iliad* 5, 889–90

Stories are told in which he comes off badly. When Hephaestus, the lame smith-god, imprisoned Hera on a magic throne, Ares failed to release her either by force or by threats. A black-figure bowl by Clitias shows him with helmet, shield and spear in an attitude of despair and dejection. In another story he was having an affair with Aphrodite, the goddess of love. Hephaestus, Aphrodite's husband, caught and held them in a metal net and brought the gods to laugh at them. Various children are attributed to him by Aphrodite: they include Eros, the love-god, and such hateful powers as Fear and Terror. In general, his mythological children are outlaws, brigands and men of violence, like Cycnus or Phlegyas. He was naturally worshipped in the militaristic state of Sparta, but even there he seems alien, and his statue was kept fettered for fear he should run away. His commonest title was Enyalius, warlike, and as such he was the subject of a special cult at Erythrae, and at Sparta received the sacrifice of a dog, whose ferocity and function as a guardian are appropriate to a war-god, and whose red colour matched the colour of iron and indeed of blood. A more surprising cult-title is Gynaecothoenas, which has something to do with women feasting; but women often play an important part in war-magic.

Ares was the god of war and the personification of all that is warlike. But other deities share in the fighting in *The Iliad*, on both sides.

These words from Zeus awoke the fury of war.
The gods went to war, raging on either side.
Hera and Pallas Athene made for the Greek fleet
with Poseidon, god of earthquakes, and Hermes,
giver of luck, renowned for his trickery.
Hephaestus went with them, triumphing in power,
lame, but with strength in his thin legs.
To the Trojans went Ares in a dazzling helmet, and with him
Phoebus with his long hair, Artemis with her arrows,
Leto, Xanthus, and Aphrodite who delights in joy . . .
The arrival of the Olympians changed the situation.
Strife arose, strong to rouse armies. Athene raised the war-cry
standing now outside the wall near the ditch,
now shouting a challenge along the ringing shore.
Ares answered from the enemy, like a dark thunderstorm,
loudly driving on the Trojans, now from the citadel,
now running along Callicolone by the Simois.
   So the blessed gods rallied the opposing forces,
forced them together, and opened up strong strife among
      themselves.
The father of gods and men thundered aloud
over their heads. Under their feet Poseidon made
the infinite earth and the mountain-summits shake.
Every ridge and peak of Ida with its many springs
trembled, the city of Troy and the Greek ships shook,
far below Aidoneus, Lord of the Dead, was frightened
and sprang from his throne with a cry of fear, scared
that Poseidon might split the earth above his head,

and reveal to mortals and immortals the extent
of those loathsome halls the gods abominate.
There was colossal tumult as the gods strove with one another.
Naturally when the lord Poseidon faced
Phoebus Apollo with his feathered arrows,
and Hera was matched to Artemis, Apollo's sister,
huntress and archeress and queen of the golden distaff,
and Leto stood opposed to Hermes, the formidable giver of luck,
and Hephaestus to the great swirling river
called Xanthus in heaven and Scamander on earth.

Homer *Iliad* 20, 31–74

The point is that everything which goes on among men goes on more mightily among the gods. Their councils are a mightier version of human councils, their wars a mightier version of human wars. In one myth, marvellously depicted on the archaic Treasury of the Siphnians at Delphi, and the Hellenistic Altar of Zeus at Pergamon, the gods unite to wear down the Giants who challenge their power.

So although Ares was the god of war, he was not alone invoked by soldiers. To the Athenians in particular their own Athene was closer and dearer. She was the goddess of wise counsel, and of peaceable arts and crafts. But she was regularly depicted with helmet, breastplate and spear. One of her great titles was Athene Promachos, the Defender, a title given by some late authorities to Phidias's great free-standing statue of her on the Acropolis at Athens, visible far out to sea as the sun's rays caught the tip of her spear. A sculptured relief shows her in mourning for Athenians who have died in war. One of the famous traditional songs of Athens was 'Pallas, sacker of cities'.

So too Apollo was in many ways the god of peaceable activities: healing, and music, and the care of flocks and herds, a law-giver, and an inspirer of philosophic thought. But he could be militant enough in defence of his own interests, as the three so-called Sacred Wars in the sixth, fifth and fourth centuries, fought to defend Apollo's shrine at Delphi from sacrilege, amply demonstrate.

Even the goddesses, as we have seen, might be soldiers, even Aphrodite, the goddess of love (though she runs away from the harsh

5

reality of war). Zeus actually says that Ares's love of strife is due to his mother Hera. But also there are, not surprisingly, goddesses who make for peace. Notable among these is Demeter, the earth-mother or grain-mother (the derivation is disputed). Corn and agriculture generally are her gifts, and with them, civilized, settled and peaceable living. It is significant that she scarcely appears in *The Iliad*, the poem of war. She has a darker side, for in tribal religion power is power, and the power to give and to withhold are one. So, just as Apollo can bring or heal plague, so Demeter can bring or heal famine. But she is in general a goddess of peace. So, naturally, is Hestia, the domestic goddess of the hearth. Men might fight for their hearths and homes, but she herself had no part in their battles. Eirene herself was a divine being, a personification of peace. In one sense she was a purely artificial construction. She has no mythology, and there is not much record of cult, though she was worshipped at Athens with appropriately bloodless sacrifices. A celebrated statue by Cephisodotus shows her holding the infant Wealth; it is a kind of sermon in stone. The same message is sung by Bacchylides, who extols wealth, and music and dance as the gifts of Eirene, yes, and sacrifices to the gods too, while the sword rests and the spider weaves his web in the shield. Euripides too in his lost *Cresphontes* included a hymn to Eirene, and Aristophanes wrote a comedy in her honour.

Perhaps the most interesting aspect of the religious dimension of peace among the Greeks may be seen in the truce enforced during the quadrennial festival of Zeus at Olympia. This, the original Olympic Games, dated from 776 B.C. The festival itself lasted five days in the late summer, but the whole of the sacred month was a period of peace, and it is probable that the truce proclaimed by the heralds of Zeus lasted for three months. During this period there was to be no internecine warfare among the Greeks, all travellers to and from Olympia were sacrosanct, and no one might bear arms within the sacred territory. During the Peloponnesian War a Spartan force bearing arms entered the sacred territory during the period of the truce; they were fined the considerable sum of two minas a head.

It should be added that both war and peace were hedged round with the solemnity of religious ritual. Sacrifice would be offered and omens taken before troops moved into battle; the casual way in which Xenophon mentions this shows that it was taken for granted (e.g. *Hellenica* 4, 2, 18; *Anabasis* 6, 4, 14–17). One of the most famous episodes pertains to the Athenian defeat at Syracuse. Nicias, after an eclipse of the moon, refused to retreat until the twenty-seven days prescribed by his religious advisers had elapsed (Thucydides 7, 50). But although the omens were taken as given, and the broad lines of their interpretation settled, some manipulation was possible. You might go on taking omens until favourable ones appeared. You might press one interpretation rather than another, as Themistocles argued that the oracular declaration that Athens would be defended with wooden walls meant ships. You might arrange for supernatural visitations, as did Pisistratus or Themistocles, though it was dangerous to carry this too far; the Spartan king Cleomenes intrigued with Delphi, and his madness was believed to be the consequence. You might challenge or allege such manipulation. Demosthenes did so and was not charged with blasphemy. But when all this is said, victory belonged to the gods, as Themistocles declared after Salamis. So did defeat. The official epitaph on Athenians who died in battle in the middle of the fifth century declares that they died by the will of some unknown demigod to warn future generations to have faith in the fulfilment of prophecy. Much the same sort of things could be adduced of the solemn sacrifices and oaths which accompanied treaties of peace.

THE ANCIENT ROMANS

The great god of classical Rome was Jupiter, Diu-piter, father Dyaus, the same Indo-European sky-god, and the Romans came to take over the Greek pantheon. The earliest stratum of Roman religion, however, seems to have consisted not in gods and goddesses, but in powers, *numina*, barely if at all personified, each with a limited function and no existence outside that function: German scholars called them *Sondergötter* or *Augenblickgötter*, gods of the twinkling of an eye. The large majority of these were associated with either agriculture or family life, on the one hand powers who controlled ploughing and reploughing, harrowing and top-dressing and dunging, harvesting and storing, on the other, the girdling of the

7

bride and the rocking of a baby's cradle. It is somewhat surprising that the other great activity of the Romans, warring, does not show a comparable crop of *numina*. There is one comparatively late but curious example. In 212 B.C. Hannibal came within sight of Rome and withdrew. Thanks were given to Rediculus Tutanus, Goer-away Saviour. It is hard to see that this godling existed on any other occasion, but there is some evidence of a cult.

The Roman god of war was Mars, and he was later identified with Ares. In early times he was also associated with agriculture, as Ares was not. This fact has been variously interpreted. Dumézil still insists on his function as a war-god; his link with agriculture lies simply in the protection of the fields from outside enemies and from plague and pestilence. Altheim thought of him as the old Italic bull-god, fierce and fertile. Philologically the most plausible explanation would make of him a storm-god, bringing rain to the fields and striking terror into enemies. Mars was a dangerous power. Until the time of the emperor Augustus he had no temple within the walls of Rome. Outside he had a temple covering the Porta Capena, and an altar within his own field, the Campus Martius, where the armies mustered. But in the ancient royal palace there was a chapel in which were kept the spears and shields sacred to Mars, spears and shields carried in ceremonial procession by his priests in March and October at the beginning and end of the campaigning season. When a consul was about to march out to war he entered this chapel and seized the shields, and either the spears or a particular spear, and shook them, saying 'Mars, wake up!'

Much of the time of the ancient Romans was spent in war, and a college of priests called fetials, twenty in number, was responsible for all ceremonials associated with peace and war; of especial importance to the ritual was a priest known as the Fulfilling Father. All declarations of war and establishment of treaties were religious rites, formal and formulaic. For example, if the Romans were demanding redress and threatening war, the Fulfilling Father would cross the frontier, cover his head with a woollen scarf, and call upon Jupiter and justice to witness to the justice of his demands. This would be done several times. Thirty-three days were then given for the demands to be met. If they were not met, he would call upon

Jupiter and the other gods to witness that the people concerned showed no justice, return to Rome for a formal political decision, and then return again to the frontier and cast a spear coated in blood across. Similarly there were formulas and rituals directed to calling the gods away from a besieged city and cursing its inhabitants. Treaties involved a second fetial who carried with him a sacred herb from the citadel of Rome with which he would touch the head and hair of the Fulfilling Father. There followed a long verse incantation, and the sacrifice of a pig with flint-knife (this shows the antiquity of the ceremony), with a curse on Rome if she broke the treaty.

As with the Greeks, sacrifices and omens were a regular prelude to battle. One commander was falsely told that the omens were good. The lie was revealed. He blandly declared that as the omens were reported as good, good they were. The liar was placed in the front line, and was punished with his life; the battle was won. But the commanding officer who, on being told that the sacred chickens would not eat (an unfavourable omen), shouted 'Then let them drink' and threw them into the sea had gone too far in the manipulation of omens and was very properly defeated. Similarly Flaminius went into the battle of Trasimene with his religious duties unfulfilled; the result was death and defeat. But Marcellus, the noted augur during the war with Hannibal, was able to manipulate the omens by keeping his curtains drawn and not seeing the bad ones, a religious Nelson-touch. The whole crisis of religiosity during the disasters inflicted by Hannibal is of particular interest. There were omens galore, an ox leaping from a third storey, a fall of pebble-rain, adultery by a vestal virgin, a temple struck by lightning, prodigies of all kinds. There were expiations of many kinds, banquets to the gods, honours to Iuventas, the deity of conscripts, and to the powers of childbirth (to provide more sword-fodder in case of a long war), the introduction of new gods (such as the Great Mother of Pessinus), the vowing of the products of the spring to Mars and Jupiter, special dedications to Jupiter, the great god of the state, dedications to Honour and Courage, even, in dire emergency, human sacrifice.

One important ritual associated with peace and war was the closing of the temple of Janus for peace and its opening for war. Janus is presumably the power of the gate or door (*ianua*). He is a god of openings and closings, worshipped on the first of the month, and in the first month after the winter solstice, January, which bears his name. It is not altogether clear why this particular ceremonial took place. Perhaps in time of war special attention had to be paid to the god of the city-gate. In time of peace this was no longer necessary.

Other gods had their part in war, Jupiter above all. It was his eagle which the Roman legions carried as their standard. His cult-titles show his importance to the soldiers – Protector (*Conservator*), Victor, Defender (*Propugnator*), Supporter (*Stator*), Avenger (*Ultor*). Later, as the Roman frontiers began to crack and break, they turned to another militant god from the east, the Unconquered Sun: in 274 C.E. the emperor Aurelian enthroned him as the great god of the Roman people, to burn up Rome's enemies.

In the last days of the Republic, when a succession of civil wars was wasting the Roman people, the Epicurean Lucretius wrote a poem to commend the tranquil, pacifistic philosophy of his master. Epicureans did not believe in gods who interfere in the affairs of men. But Lucretius at the outset of his poem invokes Venus, goddess of love, the Greek Aphrodite and the legendary mother of Aeneas, Rome's founder. He uses the old myth of Ares and Aphrodite.

> Cause the savage works of war
> to slumber and cease over land and sea.
> You alone can bless mankind with tranquil
> peace, since military Mars rules the savage
> works of war, and he often drops
> into your lap, overpowered by love's endless wound,
> and looking up with shapely neck thrown back
> gazes on you, goddess, and feeds his eagerness on love,
> and his breath hangs on your lips as he lies there.
> Goddess, bend over him with your holy body
> as he lies there, pour gentle words
> from your illustrious lips, ask peace and quiet for Rome.
>
> Lucretius, 29–40

This was a voice crying in the wilderness. But out of the wars Augustus became dominant. Now almost for the first time we find at

Rome peace personified, Pax, and the great Altar of the Augustan Peace shows some of the values cherished, the goddess Rome with her weapons laid aside, Aeneas sacrificing to the gods of hearth and home, Mother Earth with children on her lap and cattle grazing peaceably around.

Yet the commitment to peace as a religious concept was at best ambivalent. Rome may have laid her arms aside, but they are at the ready. The fourth panel shows Romulus and Remus suckled by the fierce she-wolf. Augustus was proud of the peace he had brought, but he sent his legions into Germany. The Apollo who was to shower the blessings of peace on the new régime was the Apollo who had blessed Augustus's navy in the battle of Actium. 'If you want peace, prepare for war' is a Latin epigram. The religious destiny of Rome was voiced by the former Epicurean Vergil:

> Others will beat out bronze into life more supply,
> they will indeed, and draw living looks from marble;
> will plead cases better, will trace the paths of the sky
> with a compass and tell the rising of the stars.
> You, Roman, remember to rule the nations by your
>   authority
> (there lies your skill), to give a place to Peace,
> to spare the humble, and war down the proud.
>
> Vergil *Aeneid* 6, 847–53

Rome might bring peace, but her religious destiny was in war and government.

SCANDINAVIAN RELIGION

The warriors of Scandinavia had a religion more closely and fully linked with war. Legend told of a great war among the gods themselves, between the Aesir and Vanir. This was not a war between the powers of light and the powers of darkness. It perhaps represents a conflict between two groups of tribes, each with their own gods, the Vanir representing earlier deities of Scandinavia, the Aesir coming up from Germany. *Voluspa* calls this conflict the first war in the world. It ended in stalemate, a truce and the exchange of hostages.

Although there was some differentiation of function among the Scandinavian deities the gods generally were conceived of as warriors, living in the fortress of Asgard. Thus Wotan or Odin, the All-Father, supreme among the Aesir and their commander against the Vanir, was a great soldier and conqueror, whose appearance in war spelt terror. He was lord of all wars and battles; he empowered men against their enemies. One of his names was Val-father, father of the slain. He and Freya (one of the Vanir), or perhaps Frigg, Wotan's consort, chose those out of the dead in battle who would be transported to Valhalla. Wotan's servants in this were the Valkyries, warrior-maidens, choosers of the slain, riding to battle with helmet, sword and spear, their breastplates stained with blood. These are minor goddesses, and some of their number seem to be deified mortals. They may be a divine projection to the shield-maids of ancient Germany. Wotan's gifts to men included poetry and wisdom, but many of them are concentrated upon war. Human sacrifice was offered to him as lord of life and death.

Second only to Wotan, and pre-eminent in Norway, was Thor, the Thunderer, the red-bearded god of the thunderstorm, whose symbol was the hammer. As a storm-god he had to do with the fertility of the land; he was also naturally a god of war. An ancient burlesque gives him similar functions to those of Wotan, except that Wotan receives the dead officers, and Thor the dead privates. The Norman Vikings offered him human sacrifice before sailing out on piratical expeditions.

Wotan and Thor were military gods with wider functions. Tyr or Tyw, who gives his name to Tuesday, was solely the god of battles, valiant and daring, giver of victory, inspirer of the brave; the Romans identified him with Mars. He too received human sacrifice.

The concentration on war in Scandinavian religion is remarkable. The general abode of the dead is called Hel. The sources vary somewhat, but on the whole it seems a thankless gloomy place, ruled over by Loki's dreadful daughter, also called Hel. But the dead soldiers chosen by Wotan went to Valhalla, a great hall built of spears and shields, swords and breastplates. There they ate roast boar and drank mead, and their sport was daily battle, followed by nightly resurrection and healing.

The gods themselves were regarded as subject to death. The Fenris-wolf, the Midgard serpent, the sons of Fire, the Frost Giants and the armies of Hel will come to the battlefield of Vigridr. As a result of this battle the gods and their enemies alike perish, and fire covers the world. This in the ultimate is the vision of a religion that is human life writ large. As men perish, so do the gods, but on a grander scale. But there is also a vision of a new heaven and a new earth.

THE YORUBA

These last are all religions which have ceased to exist except in so far as they have altered the historic patterns of European Christianity. As an example of a tribal religion, contemporary with ourselves but stretching far back in time (in myth to the creation of the world), and associated with a high civilization, we may take the Yoruba of West Africa.

Here there is a high god, Olodumare, creator and king, omnipotent and omniscient, all-seeing and all-wise. He has, as often with African high gods, many of the characteristics of a withdrawn god. He has no shrines and no images are fashioned of him. He governs through his ministers, the pantheon of the orişa. Each of these has his particular sphere of influence, and his cult may be more prominent in one locality than another. Thus Eşu, the high god's messenger, and a trickster god, is especially worshipped at Erin. Şango, perhaps originally a historical king, was deified as a storm-god – and later became the patron god of the Electricity Corporation. Şopona is the power of smallpox and other destructive diseases.

The god of war is Ogun. By tradition he was a hunter, and the patron god of hunters. All iron and steel is his; he is the god of blacksmiths – and, more recently, of engineers, motor mechanics and the like. It is to Ogun that thanks are given for escape from a road accident. He controls the machete which clears a path through the forest or turns a wilderness into a potential farm. But he is above all a man of blood.

13

Where does one meet him?
One meets him in the place of battle;
one meets him in the place of disputing;
one meets him in the place where rivers of blood
quench desire as a cup of water satisfies the thirsty.

When he first came down from his home on the top of the hill he was clothed in fire and wore a robe of blood. At the same time he is a protector of justice, and an oath in his name is of great solemnity. His sacred animal is the dog, and the dog is the characteristic offering to him at a time of crisis. Hunters naturally offer a simpler sacrifice, perhaps of a cock or of kola-nuts. But before the twentieth century in time of war, whether offensive or defensive, the offering would be a human being, a slave purchased with public money and honoured before his death with pomp and circumstance.

SOME GENERAL POINTS FROM
AFRICAN TRIBAL RELIGIONS

Anthropologists today are wary of generalizations about African religions, and it is certainly important to be aware of differences as well as likenesses. None the less it is posssible to trace common patterns.

War was a part of life, and under the gods. So to the Lango war is a demonstration of divine power, and to the Fon the divine is compounded of the gentleness of the mother and the strength of the soldier. The power of the storm may be greeted by the words 'The Lord is arming himself'. Tribes on entering war will pray and offer sacrifice for victory. Many tribes have war gods, like the Yoruba Ogun; the Ganda have two, Kibuka and Nnende, and the Ga have even more. Among the Bangiro the presence of their war-god Muhingo might be represented on an expedition by a special war-drum accompanied by a priest. Among the Ankore the hereditary priesthood is confined to the war-god. When the men are away on an expedition the women may offer prayer; the men will make their offering before and after. The Nandi offer a good example. A raid or expedition would be accompanied by an elder who would pray every morning 'God, grant us to drink milk.' At the same time at home the mothers of the soldiers would spit towards the sun with the words 'God, give us health.' On the return of the soldiers they themselves would hold an act of thanksgiving if successful, and an act of penitence if unsuccessful. The war-god is often, like Ogun, a god of iron, with wider and more comprehensive functions; if he is simply a war-god, then in time of peace he is left to slumber undisturbed.

Africa dances, and the religious dance was always a basic part of ritual preparation for war. The rhythmic power and precision of these dances is breath-taking. The percussive accompaniment is subtle, insistent, and passionate. The dancing is varied, and is likely to contain a core of necessary liturgical movement combined with improvisation. There is in Africa a deep-seated sense of the rhythm of the universe. Where R. W. Trine spoke of being *In Tune with the Infinite*, an African might more readily speak of being 'in time with the Infinite'. At a moment of major social crisis, such as war, this is vital. Secondly, there is in such dancing an element of ecstasy; the individual is not merely accustoming himself to the rhythms of the universe, but is swept out of himself. Thirdly (without contradicting the last), the dance is a check on alertness and physical fitness. Fourthly, the dance will contain plenty of mimic combat; a sceptical view would call this superstitious magic, a secular view would see in it practice; we might term it a religious pre-enactment of the scene of battle. Fifthly, there is involved the dedication and blessing of soldiers and weapons.

Military expeditions would often be associated with taboos. The soldier, involved with life and death, is a nexus of dangerous spiritual forces. One common expression of this, found all over the world, is the insistence that soldiers abstain from sexual intercourse. This is both to prevent the soldiers from being infected with womanly weakness, and to preserve the act of sex from bloody destruction. Among some southern African tribes the people left behind in the villages were equally bound to sexual continence; any offence would lead thorns to grow in the path of the expedition. On the return of the expedition it has been equally common for those who have taken life to require purification. Again, the Nandi offer an interesting example; a soldier who had killed would paint one side of his sword, spear and body white and the other red, and build a hut by the riverside where he would live in isolation for four days before he could return. On the last day he would drink a medicine made from the bark of a sacred tree, and drink goat's milk mixed with blood. Some of the Kavirondo tribes required the soldier to shave his head, and then perform some apotropaic ritual, such as having his body smeared with goat's dung, or hanging the head of a chicken round his neck. The Angoni would cover themselves with ashes, carry their victims' clothes for three days, and then run screaming through the village to scare away the spirits. The Basuto chief would sacrifice an ox for the purification of his army, ceremonially wash the soldiers who had killed, and anoint them with the gall of the ox to drive away the ghosts of their victims. Herero soldiers would crouch in a circle at some distance from the sacred hearth, which they could not approach until aspersed by their chief with water in which a sacred branch had been placed. It would be possible to cite many similar rituals of purification from other African tribes, as well as from areas as far apart as New Guinea and North America.

It should be added that a number of African tribes, including the Embu, Shona and Nyanja, see war as a national calamity sent by God in punishment or retribution for some offence committed by the community or its representative.

THE ARAPESH

In 1931 Margaret Mead and Reo Fortune renewed studies which they had been making in New Guinea and went for the first time to work among the Arapesh. Fortune had been working on Dobu, an island of fierce fighters; they went on to the Mundugumor, a society organized for ferocious aggression. There could have been no more acute contrast. Among the Arapesh aggressive behaviour received strong social disapproval; furthermore disapproval was directed against those who provoked aggressive behaviour in others. Men and women alike were expected to direct their lives to constructive behaviour, to helping things grow, plants, pigs, children; they were expected to nurture and cherish, help and save. Gentleness was the norm of behaviour. Indignation was socially permissible against one's own property, not that of others. There was no religious or magical sanction for warfare, though some protective ritual in the event of dispute. There were no blood feuds, and anyone roused to kill was on the whole an object of pity, not of admiration or vengeance. Disputes might arise in which the combatants declared themselves *ano'in*, that is isolated from one another. This was almost the only socially tolerated institution of divisiveness. Even so the children of the *ano'in*, themselves formally *ano'in*, would meet, and marriage between them was encouraged as a reconciling act. The man of violence had no place in Arapesh society.

Arapesh society is of course a spiritual society, though ritual provision is less highly organized than in many tribal societies. The power of the ancestors is strong. The organization of society is in small groups, often based on paternal clans. Each of these groups has a guardian-spirit or *marsalai*, visibly manifested in the form of a snake or other reptile. Supernatural power may also be shown in the form of sorcery, and violent behaviour is often attributed to sorcery; but sorcery which might result in death is socially unacceptable. The Tamberan cult, a men's religious society found in other parts of New Guinea, is one of the comparatively few cults which bring together the clans or local groups. Further, whereas in other parts of New Guinea the cult is socially divisive and creates hostilities, among the Arapesh it has become a ceremony of growth and symbolic of co-operation.

The Arapesh offer a rare example of a tribal society religiously organized for peace. Normally tribal religion embraces peace and war alike as facts of life; often it is orientated towards war. But among the Arapesh as in all basic tribal religion, the religious aspect is a dimension of the social culture; it does not determine it; or, better, it determines it from within, not from without.

SUMMARY

In tribal religion, religion is as wide as life, and all of life is religious. War has throughout human history been an integral part of the life of most societies; as such it has been regarded as a religious activity, to be surrounded with prayer, ritual, sacrifice and purification.

Polytheistic societies have often, though not always, believed in a special god of war who has to be honoured and propitiated. Gods (or goddesses) of peace as such are less widely found, but naturally the powers who preside over agriculture and over domestic life are powers who make for peace.

FOR FURTHER READING

Ferguson, J., *Religions of the Roman Empire.* Thames and Hudson 1970.

Fowler, W. W., *The Religious Experience of the Roman People.* Macmillan 1911.

Frazer, J. G., *The Golden Bough*, 12 vols. Macmillan 1911–27.

Idowu, E. B., *Olodumare: God in Yoruba Belief.* Longmans 1962.

McCulloch, J. A., *The Celtic and Scandinavian Religions.* Hutchinson 1948.

Mbiti, J. S., *Concepts of God in Africa.* SPCK 1970.

Mead, M., ed., *Cooperation and Competition Among Primitive Peoples*, 2nd edn. Boston, Beacon Press, 1961.

Nilsson, M. P., *Greek Piety*, Eng. tr. Clarendon Press 1948.

Chapter 2

ZOROASTRIANISM

ZARATHUSTRA AND HIS TEACHING

Zarathustra lived in Persia in the first half of the sixth century B.C., to take the most probable dating. He thus lived through the rise of Persian military power under Cyrus I, and probably just failed to see his capture of Babylon in 538. By this time his ideas had begun to permeate Persian society.

Not easily. Zarathustra's life has suffered many legendary accretions, and it is difficult to attain a sure picture of the man. He was living in an age of polytheism and animal sacrifice. Somehow, somewhere, he received a prophetic, visionary call to challenge both. Among the many *ahuras* and *daevas* who peopled the spiritual world, he singled out Ahura Mazda, the Lord of Light, the Wise Lord, as the one true God. He spoke out too, in compassion for the suffering of the 'bull-soul', against animal sacrifice. This challenge to the religious establishment led to opposition, persecution and exile.

To what land shall I go for refuge? Where am I to turn my steps?
I am thrust out from family and from tribe.
I find no support in my home-village,
none from my country's evil rulers.
How then, O Lord, shall I obtain your favour?

Yasna 46, 1

The prophet became an outcast, but gathered around him a fellowship known as the Friends, or the Beggars, or the Wise, clearly

19

a close-knit, dedicated group vowed to poverty. Through his own preaching and the work of his supporters his ideas spread.

First, there is one God only, Ahura Mazda, the Lord of Light, the Wise Lord, the Holy One.

Secondly, under Ahura Mazda there is a cosmic dualism. According to Zarathustra's myth, Ahura Mazda produced twin sons, Spenta Mainyu (Holy Spirit) and Angra Mainyu (Evil Spirit). They each made their choice, of good and evil respectively.

Now at the outset the twin spirits have proclaimed their character,
Good and Evil,
in thought, word and act. Between these two
the wise choose well, the foolish do not.

When these two spirits came together,
in the beginning they established life and non-life.
In the end the wicked should experience the worse fate,
the righteous enjoy the Good Mind.

Of these two, the Evil Spirit chose to commit evil acts.
The Holy Spirit, wearing the lasting robes of heaven,
joined himself to righteousness,
followed by all who love to please the Wise Lord
by good acts.

Between the two the false gods chose wrongly;
they miscalculated;
they chose the Evil Mind.
They were impatient to join themselves to Madness
and so to corrupt the life of man.

Yasna 30, 3–6

Most dualist systems have set spirit against matter, but here there is a cosmic conflict. Spenta Mainyu tends to be assimilated to Ahura Mazda, so that the conflict becomes one between God and the Powers of Darkness.

Thirdly, at Ahura Mazda's side are six other Holy Immortals. These are Asha, Cosmic Order, and Vohu Mana, Good Mind; Khshathra, the Kingdom and the defence of the Kingdom; Armaiti,

Right-Mindedness. Haurvatat, Wholeness, and Ameretat, Immortality. These are grouped in three. The first two have to do with the ruling function, with the principles of order, and the cosmic power of fire. Khshathra has to do with the military function. The last three are associated with the earth and her produce, the pastoral and agricultural functions, soil, vegetation and water. The military function is thus built into the pattern of the Immortals.

Fourthly, life is a battleground between the powers of Light and Darkness, Good and Evil, and human beings align themselves on either side by their choices. To choose righteousness is to live in accordance with Asha, Cosmic Order. The life to which men are called may be analysed under four heads. The first comprises the social virtues, truthfulness, the keeping of oaths, fair dealings, straightness, trustworthiness, honesty, and the compassionate virtues of hospitality to strangers and care for the underprivileged. This is the life in accordance with Asha, and it is Vohu Mana, Good Mind, who gives the impulse to it. The second group of virtues are the military virtues, courage, endurance and the like, associated with Khshathra. The third group has to do with what we should today call the environment, with the earth and its life and resources, the special concern of Armaiti, Haurvatat and Ameretat. To care for the earth, to look after cattle, to exterminate pests are among virtuous actions; to kill a clean animal is a sin. The last group has to do with purity, with sexual behaviour, contact with dead bodies, and the like.

Fifthly there is an ultimate eschatological conflict between the powers of Light, led by a Saviour (*Saoshyant*) who will appear in due season, and the powers of darkness. This final battle is conceived in military terms. In the end the powers of Darkness are overthrown, and the earth is renewed in unending youth and incorruption.

The idea of conflict and battle is thus central to Zoroastrian thought.

THE SACRAL KINGSHIP

The place of Khshathra is particularly important, for it led to the idea of the sacral kingship in Persia. The king enjoyed the special protection of the divine powers and was invested by them with royal fortune and kingly glory. In some magnificent rock-cut reliefs we can see Ahura Mazda handing the round of sovereignty to the monarch. The king is thus vice-gerent for the god. He is brother of the sun and moon, ruler of the world, champion of justice. He wears a royal cloak with the symbols of cosmic sovereignty. He is greeted with prostration. And he sums up in his person the three divinely blessed functions of priest-ruler, soldier, and guardian of the earth and her fruits. In the great palace of Persepolis, we see the king constantly with the god hovering in the sky above his head.

Cyrus I and Darius I, the great establishers of Persian military power, were both devout worshippers. Cyrus won his two major victories, over Croesus of Lydia which gave him power over Asia Minor, and over Nabonidus of Babylon which added Mesopotamia, Syria and Palestine. Darius's military work was mainly in frontier consolidation. Both were tolerant of the religions of their subjects, and Cyrus in consequence was hailed as Messiah by some Jews.

The earlier rulers of Media had the services of the priestly caste of the Magi, who were certainly associated with a solar cult. Tombs of the period show a winged disc (traditional for a sky-god) or a fire-altar with Magi at prayer. Cyrus no doubt worshipped a sky-god, and presumably found that the god of the Jews could be easily correlated with the god he knew. The inscription in which he records his religious policy and his entry into Babylon tells of his worship of Marduk in Babylon. This does not suggest a high monotheism; we know besides that though he might diplomatically honour Marduk, he regarded him as a symbol of Babylonian nationalism, and tried to replace him by Sin, the Moon. At Pasargadae Cyrus's tomb has something of the shape of a miniature ziggurat, a holy mountain, suitable to the worship of a sky-god. Nearby are two altars, rather as may be seen on late Sassanian coins, one a fire-altar and the other for blood-sacrifice.

The Achaemenid rulers were military monarchs. There is also strong evidence of religious concern, Darius (522–486 B.C.) built the great palaces at Susa and Persepolis, but we cannot identify in these any religious data of his reign. But on the tomb at Naqs-i-Rustam we see him standing in worship before a lighted altar. Above is a winged disc with the figure of Ahura Mazda. His successor Xerxes, in suppressing rebellion at Babylon, proscribed the cult of the *daevas* and replaced it by that of Ahura Mazda.

It is extremely hard to say how far the religion of the Achaemenids was influenced by Zoroastrianism, and how far it was traditional and, so to speak, unreformed. The prophet is not mentioned by name; the word *spenta* does not appear; there is no rigid monotheism; there are some divergences of belief and practice. None the less, the stress on Ahura Mazda and Xerxes's campaign against the *daevas* suggest not a pure Zoroastrianism, but at least the practice of the traditional religion in a way touched by Zarathustra's reforms.

The religion of the Achaemenids did not inhibit their military endeavours. But it seems to have been associated with an openness towards universalism and toleration. The king himself ruled under god, but was not a god. He appears as a semi-divine hero in combat with a lion, bull-man or monster. Darius is lifted up by his subjects, but is under the sky. The kings are under the divine protection of Ahura Mazda.

THE SASSANIANS

The conquest of Persia by Alexander led to great changes, and for three or four centuries strong elements of Hellenism are present in the culture. Even in the Arsacid period from about 200 B.C. no Mazdean literature survives, though a fire-altar appears on a coin of Vologeses IV, and we can trace some nationalist revolt against Hellenism from the first century C.E. at least. The great fire-temple at Hatra must date from about this period. But it is the period of the Sassanian monarchs which sees the sacral kingship most fully developed. Government was strong, centralized, autocratic, military, and religiously backed by the Mazdean priesthood. The king is 'one whose lineage is from the gods'; according to one tradition he is called 'brother of the sun and moon'; in coins and inscriptions he receives the title 'god'. Fire-altars appear continually on reliefs and coins. Associated with this is a revival of Persian military power, which in the third century C.E. successfully challenged and defeated the Romans. The same century saw the growth of Christianity and the emergence of Manichaeism. The conversion of Constantine to Christianity turned that religion into 'the enemy', and under Shapur II in the fourth century Christians and Manicheans are under stern persecution; military nationalism and exclusive religion are marching together. None the less the religion is not pure monotheism. The goddess Anahita remains prominent, and the story of the Christian martyr Mar Mu'ain shows that the authorities were calling the Christians to polytheistic practices. In fact there were four pre-eminent deities – Ahura Mazda (under the name of Ohrmazd), Mihr, Anahita and Vahram.

Chosroes I in the sixth century saw the establishment of a purer Mazdean military monarchy. He suppressed heresy by force, proclaimed publicly the truth of the Mazdean religion, called for the study of *The Avesta* and *The Zand*. At the same time, faithful as he was to the Mazdeans, he was in general liberal, welcomed Greek philosophers after the closure of the schools at Athens, and arranged their repatriation in a peace treaty with Byzantium when they proved uneasy in his court.

THE COMING OF ISLAM

Even before the Moslem conquest of Iran, Arab contingents in a Persian army had gone over to the new faith. The end of the Sassanian dynasty weakened public support for Zoroastrianism. The main area of survival was the south. The ninth century saw the production of the main Pahlavi literature; much of it is polemic directed against Islam, Christianity, Judaism or Manichaeism. We have the sense of a religion diverted by historical accident from political violence turning to a polemic of ideas and writing. Even in the fourth century Istachri could write, 'There is hardly a town or district in Persia from which a fire-temple is absent.' But that same century saw a disastrous return to political violence and a series of uprisings with the hope of re-establishing a Zoroastrian state in Iran; the defeat of the Shiraz revolt of 979 represents the end of Zoroastrianism as a political force in Iran, though a pocket of the ancient religion remains in the south to this day and Islam in Iran was much modified by indigenous religious traditions.

ZOROASTRIANISM

THE PARSIS

The survival of the ancient religion was otherwise dependent on those who emigrated to India before the tide of Islam. There they have lived across the centuries, on the whole peaceably. They were found in the late fifteenth century resisting forcibly the Moslem invasion. The most remarkable triumph of the Parsis was perhaps their influence on the Moghul Akbar. Akbar seems to have believed in one God, whose visible image was the sun, who was adored under the form of fire, and whose earthly representative he himself was. He introduced festivals from Zoroastrian practice but did not impose them by violence, being convinced 'that confidence in him as a leader was a matter of time and good counsel, and did not require the sword'.

On the whole, however, the Parsis were farmers and traders, far from the seats of political power. The eighteenth century saw a bitter schism between the two sects of the Qadimis and the Shahanshahis. The division was nominally over a difference in the calendar; at a deeper level, the Qadimis wanted to return to the ancient Iranian practice, the Shahanshahis were content to continue the developed practices they had reached in India. The schism was for a time marked by much violence.

The movement of Christian mission in the nineteenth century led to a counter-movement by the Parsis in defence of their faith, and the Parsis were swift to embrace western education, to develop philanthropy and social responsibility, and to assert their monotheism. It is this which gives them an influence beyond their numbers.

CONCLUSION

Zoroastrianism has many of the features of a reformed tribal religion. For much of its life it was associated with Persian nationalism. During that period it was one of the most militaristic of all the great religions. There were three reasons for this. First, as we have seen, a tribal religion of a people involved in a war will accept war as part of the religio-political pattern of life, and a reform, such as that of Zarathustra, does not necessarily touch this. Secondly, the particular nationalism, with which Zoroastrianism was associated was, almost inevitably in the historical circumstances, a military nationalism. But thirdly, there was something in the nature of Zoroastrianism itself which fostered the military qualities and attitude. Life was seen as a battle between light and darkness, and though a military metaphor may be used in a pacifistic cause, as in the Christian Paul's 'Put on the whole armour of God', many hearers take it literally, and Zarathustra and his followers were not pacifist. The sun had tended to be an encouragement to war; his rays are seen as arrows, and his power scorches and destroys. The military side of Zoroastrian belief had its influence far beyond the practitioners of Zoroastrian religion. In the third century C.E. the emperor Aurelian took the Unconquered Sun over as the great god of the Roman people, inspired by the military successes of the Sassanians. More, Constantine's religion was syncretistic between the Unconquered Sun and the Unconquered Son; Christ is seen under St Peter's, ascending in the chariot of the Sun-god. The vision of Revelation was already much influenced by Zoroastrian ideas of the ultimate conflict. Christianity has carried with it across the centuries a portion of Zarathustra's religion. Similarly, when Islam came into contact with the Zoroastrians, many Zoroastrians recognized a similar militancy and transferred their allegiance. But other aspects of their faith turned Islam in Iran into something very different in tone and mood from Islam among the Arabs.

For the sun is also universal. Light shines upon all. A religion of the power of light carries within itself a paradox. On the one hand it is militant, conquering the power of darkness. On the other it is universal, open, tolerant. Both can be seen in the story of Zoroastrianism, in Chosroes, for example, or Akbar. And this militant religion, once separated from the cause of nationalism, became a force for peace.

FOR FURTHER READING

Boyce, M., *A History of Zoroastrianism*. Leiden, 1975.

Boyce, M., *Zoroastrian Belief and Practice*. Routledge, 1978.

Duchesne-Guillemin, J., *Religion of Ancient Iran*, Eng. tr. Bombay, Tata Press, 1973.

Jackson, A. V. W., *Zoroastrian Studies*. New York, AMS Press, 1928.

Kulke, E., *The Parsees in India*. Munich, 1974.

Moulton, J. H., *Early Zoroastrianism*. Williams and Norgate 1913.

Murzban, M. M., *The Parsis in India*. Bombay, 1917.

Widengren, G., 'The Sacral Kingship of Iran' in *La Regalita Sacra* (*Numen* Supplementary Volume) 1959, pp. 242 ff.

Zaehner, R. C., *The Teachings of the Magi*. Sheldon Press 1975.

Zaehner, R. C., *The Dawn and Twilight of Zoroastrianism*. Weidenfeld 1961.

Chapter 3

HINDUISM AND JAINISM

THE STRUCTURES OF HINDUISM

Hinduism is in one sense just the religion of the Indians, the Hindus. It is a vastly extended and developed form of tribal religion. Hinduism is as wide as life. It embraces alike philosophical monism and popular polytheism, abstract thought and sacrificial ritual, world-denial and world-affirmation, the absorption of the mind and the satisfaction of the body. The Hindus themselves call it *Sanatana Dharma*, the eternal religion. It embraces a wide variety of beliefs; an atheist or agnostic may still be a Hindu. But it demands a broad acceptance of the Hindu way of life.

Such a religion both accepts life as it is, and points the way to higher things. The caste-structure suggests both the actualities of the social system and a hierarchy of values. There are four main castes (or classes – *varna* – not to be confused with the multiplicity of minor castes, *jati*, into which the system later broke): the Brahmins, the priest-rulers, the 'human gods' who are united to the power of Brahman; the Kshatriyas or warriors; the Vaishyas, or craftsmen and farmers; the Sudras, who do menial work; and beyond all of these, the despised outcastes. Thus the soldiers have a place, though not the highest, in the social hierarchy. (It will be noticed that the social structure is almost identical with that adopted by Plato in *The Republic*, where slaves, implied though not mentioned, take the place of the Sudras. The similarity is too great to be accidental; it is most reasonably explained by transmission through the Pythagoreans, whose thought has other affinities with that of India.)

28

The Brahmanic system involved sacrifice as an integral part. So a doctrine of reverence for life could not easily grow up within the system. It has to be part of a reformist movement. The Brahmins were later able to absorb it: the strength of Hinduism has been its capacity to absorb all kinds of doctrines and practices at different levels. But it came in part from the Jains and Buddhists.

In Hindu thought *dharma* is doing that which is appropriate to the circumstances in which you find yourself. In *The Mahabharata* there is an illuminating conversation between Brahmana and a humble hunter named Dharmavyadha. Dharmavyadha recognizes that his beastly profession is laid upon him in ineluctable punishment for misdeeds committed in a former existence. It is the more vital to perform conscientiously the actions appropriate to the life allocated to him, even though they involve the infliction of pain and death on others. He says:

> Men kill countless creatures that live on
> the ground when they trample them underfoot.
> The wisest and best-instructed men kill many
> creatures in various ways, even while sleeping
> or resting. Both earth and sky are full of
> living organisms which are killed by men quite
> unconsciously in their ignorance.

Mahabharata Vinaparva 207, 30

Brahmana's comment is one of encouragement: 'Since those evil actions belong to the duties of your profession, the penalty of evil *karma* will not attach to you' (215, 11).

But there are glimpses of another view. In *The Ramayana* the demon-king Ravana is dead. Hanuman, the monkey-god, wants to massacre his supporters. Sita will not let him do it – they were only obeying orders – and quotes in support the reply of the bear to the tiger:

> You should not retaliate when another does you injury. Good conduct is the adornment of those who are good. Even if those who do wrong deserve to be killed, the noble ones should be compassionate, since there is no one who does not transgress.

So in the *Manu Smriti* the principle is laid down, not so much that certain acts of injury towards others are wrong in any absolute sense, as that to refrain from them helps towards non-attachment. As this is true of sexual indulgence and drinking intoxicating liquor, so it is true of meat-eating: 'the killing of living beings is not conducive to heaven' (5, 48). The *Manu Smriti* goes beyond this. Causing harm to any living creature is put alongside purity, truthfulness and honesty in Manu's summary of the law of the four castes.

THE GITA

The Bhagavad Gita (probably an early addition to *The Mahabharata*) puts the ambivalence clearly. The hero Arjuna is ready to go to battle for the Pandavas against their cousins the Kauravas. But as the battle is about to begin, he addresses his charioteer Krishna (an avatar of the god Vishnu) and tells him that he cannot fight.

It is not right that we slay our kinsmen. . . . How can we be happy if we kill our own people. . . . Alas, what a great sin have we resolved to commit in striving to slay our own people through our greed for the pleasures of the kingdom! Far better would it be for me if the sons of Dhritarashtra, with weapons in hand, should slay me in the battle, while I remain unresisting and unarmed.

So he threw his weapons on one side (1, 26–47).

But Krishna urges him to battle, and brings two lines of argument to bear. One is that physical death does not touch the *atman*, the essential self.

Just as a person casts off worn-out garments and puts on others that are new, even so does the embodied soul cast off worn-out bodies and takes on others that are new. Weapons do not cleave this self, fire does not burn him; waters do not make him wet; nor does the wind make him dry. He is uncleavable. He cannot be burnt. He can be neither wetted nor dried. He is eternal, all-pervading, unchanging and immovable. He is the same for ever (2, 22–4)

The other line of argument is based on *dharma*.

Further, having regard for your own duty, you should not falter; there exists no greater good for a *kshatriya* (warrior) than war enjoined by duty. Happy are the warriors, Arjuna, for whom such a war comes of its own accord as an open door to heaven. But if you do not engage in this lawful battle, then you will fail in your duty and your glory, and incur sin (2, 31–3).

The virtues of non-violence are appropriate to a Brahmin, not to a *kshatriya*.

Behind this is a kind of fatalism, combined with an indifference to the corporal world. 'Even without you, all the soldiers standing armed for battle will not stay alive. Their death is foreordained by me; you are merely to be the tool' (11, 32–3). The cycle of death and rebirth is fixed: no use to struggle against the inevitable (2, 27). So *The Gita* in the end justifies action which is seemingly wrong. There are, however, strict rules of war: cavalry may go into action only against cavalry, infantry against infantry and so on. The wounded, prisoners, runaways and noncombatants are to be respected. This is something like a just war doctrine.

AHIMSA

Ahimsa, non-harmfulness or non-violence, was slow in coming into Hinduism. It appears in the *Chandogya Upanishad*. 'Austerity, almsgiving, uprightness, *ahimsa*, trustfulness – these are the gifts for the priests' (3, 17, 4). In general, however, it was the Jains and Buddhists who brought *ahimsa* into the consciousness of India. Patanjali included *ahimsa* as one of the 'restraints' for the practitioner of yoga.

The restraints are: *ahimsa*, truthfulness, abstinence from theft, continence, abstinence from greed (*Yoga Sutra* 2, 30). Pantanjali called the acceptance of these restraints 'the great vow', and asserted that they were universal and absolute, and not relative to time, space, circumstance or life-style. Later commentators, however, moved away from this absolute position, and made of *ahimsa* a relative obligation only. Thus, to take a specific example, a soldier might take his vow to do injury in battle only.

JAINISM

Jainism traces back its ancestry perhaps to the eighth century B.C., but its effective power dates from the figure of Mahavira in the late sixth and early fifth centuries. Jainism is a system of world-negation, but one in which world-negation acquires a strong ethical bent. The basis of Jain ethics is *ahimsa*. *Han* means to kill or do harm; *hims* is the desiderative form and means to desire to kill or do harm; *ahimsa* is the renunciation of the will or desire to kill or to do harm.

The origin of this commandment is ambiguous. On the one hand there is in Indian thought a strong sense of the unity of the universe; all are linked to one universal soul. There is thus a strong positive element in *ahimsa*. It is however important to see that it does not arise from compassion for the individual creature, but from a larger vision of total kinship. On the other hand there is an equally strong desire to escape from the material world; an action which did harm to a fellow-creature would be the action of one involved in the world. *Ahimsa* in origin is in short a rule of inaction rather than a rule of action. 'One may not kill, ill-use, insult, torment, or persecute any kind of living being, any kind of creature, any kind of thing having a soul, any kind of being. That is the pure, eternal enduring commandment of religion which has been proclaimed by the sages who comprehend the world' (*Ayaramgasutta*).

So the Jains gave up hunting; they abandoned meat-sacrifice; they became vegetarians. They even gave up agriculture, since it seemed impossible to dig the soil without damage to the minute living organisms which inhabit it. The Jain monks try to filter their breath through a veil so as to avoid damage to the insects in the air.

Negative and positive go hand in hand. Naturally, no human being is without compassion, and the negative act leads to the positive. Out of the refusal to take life reverence for life grows. Out of non-action emerges compassionate non-action.

According to the Jains, the soul (*jiva*) is entangled in matter and needs to be released. *Karma* is the hold which matter has on the soul.

Selfish or cruel acts intensify the grip of *karma*, good deeds are neutral, unselfish acts of suffering voluntarily undertaken loosen *karma*'s hold.

> One should know what binds the soul, and, knowing, break free from bondage.
> What bondage did Mahavira declare, and what knowledge did he teach to remove it?
> He who grasps at even a little, whether living or lifeless, or consents to another doing so, will never be freed from sorrow.
> If a man kills living things, or slays by the hand of another, or consents to another slaying, his sin goes on increasing.
>
> *Sutrakritanga* 1, 1, 1

So the Jain monk will not even light a fire or lamp, for fear of destroying insects, and because of respect for the living fire itself.

> The man who lights a fire kills living things,
> While he who puts it out kills the fire;
> Thus a wise man who understands the law
> Should never light a fire.
> There are lives in earth, and lives in water,
> Hopping insects leap into the fire,
> And worms dwell in rotten wood,
> All are burned when a fire is lighted.
>
> *Sutrakritanga* 1, 6

Jainism has, however, in contradiction to its tenets, produced men of violence as prolifically as other religions. Thus in the tenth century there was a leading Jain named Chamunda Raya Karnataka, a heroic soldier who stormed the seemingly impregnable fortress of Ucchangi, served under Gangas, and routed the enemy 'like an elephant putting a herd of deer to flight'. Again in the twelfth century we find a brilliant company of Jain military commanders, no less than eight of them serving King Vishnuvardhana. Nor did they by any means confine themselves to defensive campaigns but engaged deliberately in aggressive conquest. The most famous of these was Ganga Raja. His parents were devout Jains, as were his wife and family. So was he himself up to a point, but the Jain historian decorously suggests that he was a soldier first and Jainism took second place to this. He was called 'the terrifier of his enemies, the purifier of his family, the raiser up of the Kingdom of Vishnuvardhana'; a contemporary courtly writer compares the King to the storm-god and Ganga to his thunderbolt. Ganga's son Boppa, though brought up in the highest principles in the Jain religion, was also a soldier. Later in the century came another outstanding figure, Hulla, royal minister, general, and 'restorer of the temples' – politician, soldier and man of religion.

Equally the true Jain witness was also kept strong. In the twelfth century the poet Hemachandra hymned *ahimsa* to King Kumarapala:

Ahimsa is like a loving mother of all beings.
Ahimsa is like a stream of nectar in the desert of *Samara*.
Ahimsa is a course of rainclouds to the forest-fire of suffering.
The best herb of healing for the beings tormented by the disease
called the perpetual return of existence is *Ahimsa*.

INDIAN HISTORY

Indian history has not been lacking in wars, and there has been little in Hindu religion to inhibit this. Thus the Gupta empire (320–484 C.E.) has been called the Golden Age of Hinduism. It was a period of prosperity; a period of education; a period in which free health services were available to the poor; a period of law and order; a period of culture and literature, which saw the great poet and dramatist Kalidasa. Buddhism was influential and the Hindu rulers were tolerant of it and allowed it to influence legislation: capital punishment, for example, was unknown even for rebellion. But Chandragupta, the founder of the dynasty, who was crowned by Brahman rites in 320, and his son Samudragupta were soldier-monarchs and conquerors.

Again, the Rajputs, who were a dominant feature of Indian life from the ninth century onwards, claimed to be descendants of the ancient *kshatriya* caste. They called themselves the 'sword arm of Hindustan', protecting the Hindu religion, the Brahmins and the laws by force of arms. They were initiated into their calling by the ceremonial binding on of the sword. They fought one another for their brides. They fought among themselves clan against clan. They fought external enemies. And when one of them died in battle, his widow died on his pyre with him.

Again, the coming of the Muslim conquerors was resisted violently by the Hindus in defence of their land, society and religion. Outside Peshawar in 1008 Anandpal formed a confederacy to oppose the invasion of Mahmud, and was all but successful. Fifteen years later the image-breaker, as Mahmud was called, swept down upon Śiva's great temple in Kathiawar. The Hindus fought desperately to save the temple: according to the records 50,000 died in battle, and many thousands more were drowned. In 1191 Muhammad Ghori bore down on Delhi. The Hindu leader was the romantic Prithvi Raj Rahtor. He achieved a rare unanimity among the Indian princes and repelled the invaders, only to succumb the following year. It has been suggested that Jain and Buddhist pacifism weakened the Hindu will to resist the Muslims. But there is little sign of this. Buddhist influence was now negligible. Jainism was stronger. But the Hindus were ready enough to fight; they were too busy fighting one another to be militarily effective.

Fighting between Hindus and Moslems continued across the centuries. In 1504 Babur, 'the lion', founder of the Moghul empire, took Kabul. Twenty years later he invaded India. In 1525 he took Agra and Delhi. The Rajputs under their one-eyed, one-armed, scarred commander Rana Sangha Sisodia, rallied to throw him out. Instead they themselves were put to the sword. Babur won, but left the Hindu princes in peace so long as they paid their tribute. His successors first conquered the Rajputs and then won them over by conciliation. A Rajput princess was mother to the great Jahangir. There was trouble in the south too. At Vijayanagar, Rama Raja, a usurper and autocrat, wantonly offended the sultans, who attacked him in 1564. The battle of Talikot which ensued has been called the most desperate battle in the history of southern India; it was won by the Muslim artillery. The Hindu ranks broke, and three days later the Muslims entered the city, plundered it and left it desolate.

Again, in 1769 the Hindu rulers of Rajputana used military aggression to occupy the lower slopes of the Himalayas, creating the state of Nepal, which itself acquired a notable reputation for the quality of its fighting men.

It is needless to continue. After the British entered India Hindu soldiers formed a significant part of the British army. The occasion of the Indian Mutiny was the offence given to troops at the alleged greasing of cartridges with cow fat. The independence of India and Pakistan saw what was effectively a civil war, in which Muslims and Hindus alike were massacring one another, and when Gandhi intervened for peace it was a Hindu who assassinated him. Hindus serve today in the Indian Army, an army which has made a notable contribution to United Nations peace-keeping action.

GANDHI

It was Gandhi (1869–1948) more than any other individual who brought *ahimsa* into the active moral consciousness of Hinduism. He was a strong but realistic exponent of *ahimsa*. He was ready, for example, to end the life of a calf which was in suffering, thus offending both Hindu orthodoxy and his own radical supporters. Similarly though reluctantly, he permitted the killing of dangerous snakes or of monkeys which were a menace to crops.

At the same time he began to work out the relevance of *ahimsa* to politics. But Gandhi, unlike many earlier exponents of *ahimsa*, was world-affirming, not world-denying; he fostered not non-action but non-violent action. In working this out he went outside the Hindu tradition to Jesus, and to Christian and post-Christian European and American practitioners of non-violence, notably Thoreau, Ruskin and Tolstoy.

Gandhi worked out his political stand in opposition to discriminatory legislation in South Africa between 1906 and 1914. His methods included civil disobedience, pass-burning, withdrawal of labour, picketing, non-violent demonstration, and the willingness to suffer without retaliation. On returning to India in 1914 he applied similar methods to remedying economic and social injustice, and to a 25-year-long struggle for Indian independence.

He won notable victories for poverty-ridden tenants in Champaram and underpaid millhands in Ahmedabad. Later his methods were responsible for the breaking of a situation of social injustice at Vykom in Mysore where untouchables were not allowed to pass a particular temple, and suffered beatings and stood in the rainy season till they were up to their necks in water and mud, rather than give up their non-violent protest. Gandhi was responsible for the non-co-operation campaign with the British after the Amritsar massacre. It was not an unqualified success, and when his followers lacked his discipline and broke out in violence he called off the campaign, and himself suffered arrest and imprisonment. This was characteristic. He himself wrote cheerfully, 'Non-co-operation, though a religious and strictly moral movement, deliberately aims at the overthrow of the government and is therefore legally seditious.' Again, in 1930 came the famous Salt March, when Gandhi walked 241 miles to the sea to pick up salt in defiance of the government's Salt Laws, and was again arrested. Others carried on the civil disobedience, with Mrs Sarojini Naidu and Gandhi's son Manilal in the lead. They suffered beatings without defence or protest. British political power in India lasted for seventeen more years. But, as Louis Fischer put it, 'When the Indians allowed themselves to be beaten with batons and rifle butts and did not cringe they showed that England was powerless and India invincible. The rest was merely a matter of time.'

Gandhi's mature philosophy of non-violent resistance saw a strategy embracing five stages: constitutional approaches; if these should fail, agitation to arouse awareness, or (as it would today be called) conscientization; if this failed to move those in power the next stage would be the issuing of an ultimatum, designed to shock them into thinking again; failing this, the next, astonishing stage was spiritual preparation and self-purification, prayer and fasting, the fostering of an awareness of the protesters' own responsibility for the situation, the elimination of self-interest; finally came direct non-violent action. If a non-violent campaign broke out into violence Gandhi was always ready to withdraw from it.

Gandhi was very clear about means and ends. He once said that 'we have always control over the means and never on the ends'. But he insisted on an organic connection between means and end. 'The means may be likened to a seed, the end to a tree; and there is just the same inviolable connexion between the means and the end as there is between the seed and the tree.' We may never say that the end justifies the means; that is blasphemy. On the contrary, the means determine the end. Gandhi saw in *ahimsa* a positive moral force.

I . . . justify entire non-violence, and consider it possible in relations between man and man and nations and nations; but it is not 'a resignation from all real fighting against wickedness'. On the contrary, the non-violence of my conception is a more active and more real fighting against wickedness than retaliation whose very nature is to increase wickedness. I contemplate a mental, and therefore a moral opposition to immoralities. I seek entirely to blunt the edge of the tyrant's sword, not by putting up against it a sharper-edged weapon, but by disappointing his expectation that I would be offering physical resistance. The resistance of the soul that I should offer instead would elude him. It would at first dazzle him, and at last compel recognition from him, which recognition would not humiliate him but would uplift him.

Non-violence in Peace and War 1, 44

He linked *ahimsa* with *satya* (truth) and *tapasya* (asceticism). Gandhi liked to use the positive term soul-force or truth-force (*satyagraha*). He claimed three things for his way of *satyagraha*. First, it was distinctive and natural to our humanity. Non-violence is the law of our species as violence is the law of wild animals: our spirit calls us to a higher way. Secondly, this was not visionary cloudiness, but practical idealism: it was not a way for saints only, but for ordinary people. Thirdly, dynamic non-violence means conscious suffering, not meek submission to the will of the evil-doer, but meeting his will with the whole of one's soul working under the very law of our being.

Gandhi claimed that the fight of which Krishna speaks in *The Gita* was a spiritual battle, and that the battlefield lay inside Arjuna. He said of *The Gita* that under the guise of physical warfare it described the duel that perpetually went on in the hearts of mankind, and that physical warfare was brought in merely to make the description of the internal duel more alluring. He used to assert that the central teaching of *The Gita* was selfless action (*anasakti*). There are certainly grounds for stressing the importance of *anasakti* in *The Gita*, but Gandhi's exclusive emphasis on it is not the natural interpretation, and a more natural reading would suggest that the man who frees himself from self-centredness and is totally devoted to the divine can enter fully even into war in the confidence that he is acting in accordance with *dharma*. Further Gandhi insisted that *anasakti* necessarily embraced *ahimsa*, non-violence, and that the man who is free from self cannot do violence to another. Selfless action and violent action are incompatible with one another. True *dharma*, even the *dharma* of a *kshatriya* or member of the warrior-class, must always be non-violence. Gandhi, however, said:

Everyone who has studied the *Gita* must needs find out his own solution. And although I am going now to offer mine, I know that ultimately one is guided not by the intellect but by the heart. The heart accepts a conclusion for which the intellect subsequently finds the reasoning. Argument follows conviction. Man often finds reasons in support of whatever he does or wants to do.

Gandhi's position sometimes seems ambiguous, because he encouraged people to follow the highest light they had received. It was better to be a sincere soldier than an insincere pacifist, and he told the Pathans of the north-west province in 1938 that they would do better to stick to violence, unless they were sincerely convinced that non-violence was the superior method of overcoming evil. Such a position was not really ambiguous. Gandhi's own commitment was clear, and his certainty that in the end non-violence alone was right.

Rabindranath Tagore, not one who always agreed with Gandhi, paid him a notable tribute in a letter to C. F. Andrews.

The truth that moral force is a higher power than brute force will be proved by the people who are unarmed. Life, in its higher development, has thrown off its tremendous burden of armour and a prodigious quantity of flesh, till man has become the conqueror of the brute world. The day is sure to come when the frail man of spirit, completely unhampered by air fleets and dreadnoughts, will prove that the meek are to inherit the earth.

It is in the fitness of things that Mahatma Gandhi, frail in body and devoid of all material resources, should call up the immense power of the meek that had been waiting in the heart of the destitute and insulated humanity of India.

Letters to a Friend 127

Since Gandhi's death successive governments have not followed his methods, though individuals such as Vinoba Bhave have continued to proclaim and practise his way of peace.

FOR FURTHER READING

HINDUISM

Bondurant, Joan, *Conquest of Violence*. Princeton, 1958.

Gandhi, M. K., *Non-violence in Peace and War*, 2 vols. Ahmedabad, 1948–9.

Morgan, K. W., ed., *The Religion of the Hindus*. New York, George Ronald, 1953.

Radhakrishnan, S., *The Hindu View of Life*. New York, Macmillan, 1927.

Schweitzer, A., *Christianity and the Religions*. Eng. tr. Allen and Unwin, 1923.

Schweitzer, A., *Indian Thought and its Development*. Eng. tr. Black, 1936.

Shridharni, K., *War without Violence: A Study of Gandhi's Method and its Accomplishments*. New York, Harcourt, 1939.

Zaehner, R. C., *Hindu Scriptures*. Dent, 1966.

JAINISM

Bhargava, D., *Jaina Ethics*. Delhi, Motilal Banarsidus, 1968.

Saletone, B. A., *Medieval Jainism*. Bombay, n.d. (1938).

Stevenson, S., *The Heart of Jainism*. Oxford, 1915.

Chapter 4

BUDDHISM

THE BUDDHA

Gautama, to give him his family name, or Siddhartha, his personal name, was born about 560 B.C. into a ruling family in northern India, and grew up among all the normal prejudices and practices of the upper class; one scholar has suggested that *mutatis mutandis* it was like being raised in a Scottish castle. According to one story a seer said that he was destined to be either a world-ruler, or, if he should set eyes in succession upon a man decrepit with age, a man afflicted with plague, a dead body, and a monk, he would be a homeless wanderer. His father tried unavailingly to shield him from these portents. He saw them, and renounced political and military power.

He went in search of enlightenment. He sought it first in Hindu philosophy, and then in a ruthless asceticism. Neither brought him liberation. Then as he sat in meditation under the bo-tree (*ficus religiosa*) Truth came. Life is suffering; to extinguish suffering we must extinguish desire or attachment to the world. But here came an apparent contradiction. He faced the temptation to go straight to Nirvana, to the heaven-haven which is liberation from the world and the annihilation of desire, and saw it as a temptation to be overcome. He looked compassionately with the all-seeing eye of Enlightenment, and saw men whose sight was darkened. He was the lotus who had emerged from the waters and flowered. But other potential flowers lay beneath the surface. So for forty-five years he went about India proclaiming his gospel of salvation, till in the Great Decease, through a series of ecstasies, he passed into Nirvana.

41

Buddhism is thus a world-renouncing religion which none the less lays stress on the service of others in this world to help them to escape. And the Buddha's way was a middle way between sensuality and extreme asceticism and mortification of the flesh.

THE THREE JEWELS

The Three Jewels of Buddhism are:

> I go to the Buddha for refuge.
> I go to the Doctrine for refuge.
> I go to the Community for refuge.

Buddhism does not believe in a God as do, say, Judaism or Islam. There is no original creator-god. There is nothing permanent in the world, and there is no eternal permanent god. All beings are subject to coming-to-be and passing-away. There are gods, and much popular Buddhism depends on them. They are impermanent beings, subject to natural law, with a beginning and an ending. They are not creators; they are not almighty, and they have no power to liberate. Nagarjuna actually said:

> We know the gods are false and have no concrete being;
> Therefore the wise man does not believe them.
> The fate of the world depends on causes and conditions;
> Therefore the wise man does not rely on gods.

Beyond the gods stand the Enlightened Ones, and especially the Buddha himself, who is called 'the god beyond the gods'. But he is not the creator; he is not almighty; he did not determine the laws of the universe and cannot alter them. He is the Enlightened One who enlightens others. He thus receives veneration; his familiar image stands in the temples and flowers are offered before it but he himself is in the blissful non-being of Nirvana.

His instrument of redemption is the Doctrine or Teaching (*Dharma*). This consists in the Four Noble Truths:

1   The Noble Truth about suffering, that all life is suffering.
2   The Noble Truth about the origin of suffering, that it comes from *tanha*, desire, attachment to this world, the will to live.

3 The Noble Truth about the destruction of suffering, that it comes from the extirpation of desire.

4 The Noble Truth about the way to this, that it is an Eightfold Path. The Eightfold Path is thus the guide to life. It consists in:

1 Right understanding: a full grasp of the Eight Noble Truths. We can live rightly only if we grasp what life is really like.

2 Right thought: a pure and compassionate mind, free from anything which would obstruct spiritual progress.

3 Right speech: a bridge between right thought and right action, a speech which is wise and kindly, reconciling not provocative, peaceable not inflammatory, open not dogmatic, free from lying, frivolous gossip, backbiting and the like.

4 Right action: observance of the Five Precepts. These are

   (i) not to kill, but to practise a love which does no harm to any. This is the principle of *ahimsa*, non-violent action, or non-harm, which is found at this same period in Jainism; we cannot be quite certain where it originated.

   (ii) not to take that which is not given (obviously not to steal, but the precept goes further), but to show a charitable generosity.

   (iii) not to commit sexual misconduct of any kind. For monks and nuns this means celibacy, for the laity it means faithfulness and chastity, and the avoidance of fornication and adultery. It also means avoiding overstimulation of the sexual appetite, and the practice of self-control.

   (iv) not to speak falsehood, but to be sincere, honest and truthful.

   (v) not to consume intoxicants or drugs, but to be alert to the need for self-discipline.

5 Right vocation. The vocation of monks and nuns is determined already. The laity must not follow a profession harmful to others, such as the arms trade, the slave trade, butchering, the liquor trade, dealing in poison, nor any remaining counter to the Five Precepts and other principles of right, such as those involving deceit, magic or usury. Professional calling should not be determined by monetary profit.

6   Right effort, directed to the Ten Perfections: (i) generosity, (ii) morality, (iii) renunciation, (iv) wisdom, (v) energy, (vi) patience, (vii) honesty and truthfulness, (viii) determination, (ix) lovingkindness, (x) equanimity.

7   Right-mindfulness, constant alertness about the body, its feelings, the mind, its ideas. This nourishes the Seven Factors of Enlightenment: (i) mindfulness, (ii) study of the Doctrine, (iii) energy, (iv) rapture, (v) tranquillity, (vi) concentration, (vii) equanimity.

8   Right concentration, a single-minded devotion to a wholesome object.

The third jewel is the Community (or Order). This includes monks and nuns on the one hand and laity or adherents on the other. The laity are expected to believe the Doctrine, to follow the Precepts and the way of life, and to support the monks. They cannot expect to proceed directly to Nirvana, but can hope for a higher reincarnation. The monks and nuns have a stiffer discipline but a higher goal. The Community is of major importance for social thought. In the first place it cut right across and made irrelevant the caste system of contemporary Hinduism. It thus achieved something of a practical revolution. Buddhist writers describe this as *gotrabhu*, meaning that it involves a change of clan or tribal allegiance. Buddhists become members of the Buddha's clan. This in principle breaks down all national and tribal barriers, and establishes a universal community. Secondly, some Marxist interpreters have seen the Buddhist community as the only possible answer in that age to a competitive cut-throat individualism. It was, in the Marxist view, in the end an illusory solution, because it was not based on sound economic arguments and analysis, and because it was, in some sense, a religious answer. Still, it did give an experience of collective living, and it did break through the class structure. Thirdly, it seems that towards the end of his life the Buddha linked the Community with some ideas of republicanism. King Ajatasattu intended to attack the republican Vajji, and consulted the Buddha. He declared that if the Vajji continued to meet in their tribal assemblies, following the principles of consensus, honoured their elders and held to their traditions, they would continue to prosper. He also said that exactly the same thing was true of the Community of the Buddhists (*Maha Parinibbana Sutta* 1, 38; 2, 30). The most interesting part of this story is that despite the Buddha's words, the king fought and beat the Vajji. The Buddha's prophecy was unfulfilled; that it was preserved shows that it was of real importance, and it may well be that he saw in the Community what one might term the true politic.

PRECEPTS FOR LIVING

Buddhism offers many more rules for monks and laity, both general and detailed. In general it would be true to say that the ethic is self-centred. A disciple is expected to follow his own salvation rather than the needs of others; he will seek to serve the needs of others because this is a part of his own 'effort', of his own path to salvation. It is not a matter of love.

> From love comes grief, from love comes fear; he who is free from love knows nothing of either grief or fear.
>
> *Dhammapada* 215

So Ananda's personal devotion to the Buddha stood in the way of his full enlightenment till after the Buddha's death. It is also true to say that Buddhism is ultimately an escape. Work is even described as an obstruction to spiritual progress (*Visuddhi-magga* 94). In one story the Brahmin Bharadvaja at his ploughing sees the Buddha begging, and says:

> I, O ascetic, plough and sow, and eat only when I have ploughed and sown. You, O ascetic, also should plough and sow, and eat only when you have ploughed and sown.
>
> *Suttanipata* 1, 4

But the Buddha was proud of not doing manual labour in this way.

Ironically, however, Buddhism has almost more practical precepts than any other religion. The laity are organized in every relationship of life, husbands and wives, teachers and pupils, parents and children, employers and employees: each relationship is governed by mutual duties. The Buddha laid obligations on kings and ministers, rich and poor, business men and labourers. The monastic rules include minute dispositions about washing one's clothes, sleeping on the right side, living outside towns, not speaking with the mouth full, not eating gluttonously. The monk, in addition to following the Five Precepts, must not eat untimely food; attend dance, drama or music; use garlands, perfumes or decorative adornments; lie comfortably; or possess money. Later, 250 more prohibitions were added. Their ceremonial reading twice a month is the occasion for confession.

The fundamental virtues are benevolence (towards all beings at all times), compassion, joy and equanimity. The basic rules of social behaviour are well presented in *The Dhammapada*:

> Anger must be overcome by the absence of anger;
> Evil must be overcome by good;
> Greed must be overcome by liberality;
> Lies must be overcome by truth.

These rules negate any idea that evil has to be met by evil.

The monk has three fundamental rules. First, he has no property except the nine ritual objects, three articles of clothing, a razor, needles, filter, fan, sash and begging-bowl. He lives by the generosity of others; mendicancy is a discipline which keeps pride at arm's length; he may not beg or give thanks for what he receives. He eats one meal a day, in the morning; after midday all food is strictly forbidden.

Secondly, he must renounce all violence, all killing, all bloodshed. Buddhist belief in reincarnation is part of the sense of compassion for all living creatures. There is a unity among living beings. Love of oneself entails love of all; love of all is the true love of oneself. In *The Udana* the Enlightened One says:

> My thought has wandered in all directions throughout the world. I have never yet met with any thing that was dearer to anyone than his own self. Since to others, to each one for himself, the self is dear, let him who desires his own advantage not harm another.

The monk will therefore refuse to kill for meat, and some of the stricter sects include milk and eggs in the prohibition, though fish is sometimes permitted. The taking of human life is, of course, completely proscribed.

Thirdly, he must be celibate. Buddhism was from early days male-dominated, and it is full of such saws as 'Traffic with women is the ruin of men.' However, the Enlightened One stated that women might obtain enlightenment, and in some parts there are nunneries as well as monasteries.

WAR AND VIOLENCE

The Buddhist attitude to war and violence derives from the first of the Five Precepts, incumbent on monks and laity alike, not to take life nor to be party to the taking of life. In the broadest sense, life applies to all sentient beings from insects to human. beings. The Buddha has a characteristic saying: 'Everyone is afraid of violence; everyone likes life. If one compares onself with others one would never take life or be involved in the taking of life' (*Dhammapada* 130). This applies equally to war, murder, the killing of animals for food and ritual sacrifice. In a well-known story a Brahmin named Kutadanta asked the Buddha's advice about the appropriate sacrifice for the expression of a rich and varied gratitude. The Buddha commented that animal-sacrifice was cruel and caused suffering; he suggested almsgiving, the endowment of monasteries. But the best sacrifice of all was obedience to the Five Precepts (*Dighanikaya* 1, 128). In general the best sacrifice is the sacrifice of selfish desire.

For killing to be a sin there are five conditions: (i) the fact or presence of a living being; (ii) the knowledge that the being is a living being; (iii) the intention to kill; (iv) the use of appropriate means (analysed into six: bare hands, an order to others, weapons or instruments, trapping, magic, mind-force); (v) the death. If any one of these is absent, it is an accident, not a sin. But the injunction is absolute: 'Do not kill a living being. You should not kill or condone killing by others. You should abandon the use of violence. You should not use force either against the strong or against the weak' (*Suttanipata* 394). The consequence of taking life is an inferior, gloomy, sorrowful reincarnation. At best 'he who destroys the life of any being may, in his next birth, meet death unexpectedly while in the prime of life, even though he is possessed of all the amenities of life, wealth and beauty like Makaraddhaja (the Sanskrit equivalent of Adonis)' (*Telakatahagatha* 78).

The way to overcome violence is by cultivating benevolence or lovingkindness (*metta*). The means to this is meditation. It is essential to find a quiet spot free from distractions, and to sit in a relaxed position. Then the discipline should begin by concentrating on oneself:

> May I be free from enmity,
> May I be free from ill-will,
> May I be free from distress,
> May I keep myself happy.

But this is only an aspect of the total unity of all beings. So: 'May all beings be free from enmity, affliction and anxiety, and live happily. May all breathing things, all who are born, all individuals of whatever kind be free from enmity, affliction and anxiety, may they live happily' (*Patisambhida* 2, 130). The next step is to develop *metta* towards a teacher by concentrating on good things received from him and concentrating on the thought that he may be free from enmity, ill-will and distress. Then, but only then, can one pass to the same for a close friend; then for a person to whom one is neutrally disposed; and finally for an enemy. It is important not to start from anyone with whom one is closely involved in love or hatred.

A second aspect of such meditation is directed to overcoming resentment or hostility caused by a wrong in the past. Here the Buddhists recommend starting from the development of *metta* and positive good will. If this fails, the second step is concentration on the Doctrine:

> In those who harbour such thoughts as 'He abused me, he struck me, he overcame me, he robbed me' – hatred never ceases.
> In those who do not harbour such thoughts hatred will cease.
> Hatred never ceases by hatred in this world; through non-enmity it comes to an end. This is an ancient law.

Some do not think that all of us here one day will die; if they did, their dissension would cease at once (*Dhammapada* 3–6).

The monk liberates himself from resentment by cultivating lovingkindness, compassion and equanimity; by ignoring the offender, and by reflecting that his actions are his own (*Anguttaranikaya* 3, 185). If this does not work the third step is to concentrate on the good qualities of the offender. The fourth is to realize that his action has not harmed your inner being, but your resentment will do so. The fifth is to develop this by self-examination, and meditation on the relations between action and consequence. As the Buddha put it in a sermon, if you spit into the wind, your spittle soils your own face. Sixthly, it is good to concentrate on the positive qualities of self-control shown by the Master himself. Seventhly, it is useful to remember the endless round of birth and death. 'Monks, it is not easy to find a being who has not formerly been your mother or your father, your brother or your sister, your son or your daughter' (*Samyutta Nikaya* 2, 189). Next comes concentration on the advantages of *metta*. Then a kind of *reductio ad absurdum*, known as the resolution into the elements. 'What am I angry with? The hairs of this head? The earth or air or fire or water which compose the hairs?' and so on. 'When one tries resolution into the elements, one's anger finds no foothold like a mustard-seed on the point of an awl or a painting on the air.' If this all fails, then the best method is to make some constructive act such as giving a gift to the offender.

Plainly all this is a personal morality rather than a group morality. There are two reasons for stressing it here. First, Buddhism starts from a personal ethic, from the need for personal liberation, and in the end all derives from this and gives way to this. If this is so, the same principles of behaviour will apply in relation to nations as to individuals. Tribe A is in dispute with tribe B. All that is written above applies to every individual member of tribe A who will listen to the Buddha's gospel of salvation, and applies to him absolutely without qualification. He will in fact not go to war. Second, contemporary concern for non-violence embraces a whole non-violent life-style, and is deeply exercised over non-violent training. The Buddhists have had millennia of non-violent training.

THE BRAHMAJALA-SUTRA

One of the most unequivocal statements of Buddhist pacifism may be found in *The Brahmajala-sutra*. Unfortunately the date and provenance of this work are a highly controversial matter. *The Brahmajala-sutra* insists that children of the Buddha may take no part of any kind in war. They must have nothing to do with lethal weapons. They may not participate in revolts, rebellions or uprisings; they may not even participate in embassies; it is a sin even to watch a battle. They may not kill either directly or indirectly; they may not give their assent or approval to killing; they may not be a party to killing in any way. Their minds must be filled with charity and submission. 'Murder', the taking of life, directly or indirectly, privately or publicly, is requited with excommunication.

AŚOKA

One of the most interesting episodes in the history of Buddhism relates to the Maurya emperor Aśoka (*c*. 270–232 B.C.). Aśoka had been a military imperialist, who had expanded his dominion by ruthless aggression. Even if we assume that stories of the wickedness of his youth were sermon-material rather than stern history, he was at best a typical military ruler. He was converted to Buddhism in later life and came to repent of a career based on bloodshed. One of his own rock-carved edicts records the conversion. There was a victorious battle; thousands of the enemy were killed. 'Then arose his sacred majesty's remorse; then began his love of the Doctrine and zealous protection of the law of piety.'

According to some accounts he became a monk. This seems unlikely, as he certainly remained ruler. But he was a changed ruler. He set himself to foster righteousness, social justice and peace, and put up decrees, records and exhortations, laying down the principles of his Buddhist reforms all over his vast empire. 'Whatever exertion I make, I strive only to discharge the debt that I owe to all living creatures.' We do not find in his edicts any account of Nirvana, or the Four Noble Truths, or the Eightfold Path. But we find it stated that the supreme value and sacredness of life should be firmly strengthened. There is stress on speaking the truth, on family affection, on generosity, on hard work, on abstinence from taking life, on compassion, on asceticism. He established something like a welfare state. 'The King is like your father. He cares for our welfare as much as he cares for himself.' He built rest-houses and shelters, hospitals and veterinary establishments. He established a system of state medical care for men and animals, importing herbal remedies, when these were not readily available. We also find what we should today term care for the environment, the growing of trees and the development of the water supply. D. D. Kosamli expressed it well: 'With Aṣoka the social philosophy expressed in the sixth century Magadhan religions (Buddhism and Jainism) had at last penetrated the state mechanism.' He proclaimed religious tolerance; he called for obedience to elders, respect for teachers, honour for ascetics, truth-telling and reverence for life. From being a man of war he became a man of peace. From being a noted huntsman, he prohibited blood-sports, and the killing of animals for sacrifice, and even turned aside from the eating of meat, refusing to serve it at court banquets.

BUDDHISM AS A FORCE FOR PEACE

Another example of the impact of Buddhism on a society organized for war can be seen in central Asia. Maurice Percheron has written: 'In actual fact, Buddhism did modify the warlike character of the Mongols and the Tibetans: from the peaceful bearing of the Soyots and Khalkhas of the present day, one can scarcely imagine that these are genuine descendants of the fierce horsemen of Genghis Khan.' There is no doubt that Buddhism greatly reduced the will to fight among Mongols and Tibetans. In the eighth century a Turkish Khan was advised to keep away from Buddhists if he wished to remain militarily strong; in the thirteenth century Kublai Khan used Buddhism as a means of keeping Tibet militarily neutral.

Something similar can be discerned in China despite the rebellious militarism of some of the monks. Thus in 536 C.E. we see a twenty-year-old officer resigning from the army to become a religious. In 625 or thereabouts Fou Yi rebuked the Buddhists for avoiding military service. In 706 Li Kiao voiced the view that if all conscripts became Buddhists he would have no soldiers left. Yuan Tchen (779–831) declared that the Buddhists used their religion as an excuse for shirking their military duty.

PARTICIPATION IN WAR

Both Theravada and Mahayana history, however, contain examples of participation in war. In Ceylon King Duttha-Gamani marched to war with a relic of the Buddha as his banner. Monks enlisted at his side. One became a general. He was disturbed at the number of enemy lives he had taken. His advisers comforted him with the news that only one and a half human beings had lost their lives: the rest were criminals and no better than animals. In Tibet the king Glan Durma, notoriously hostile to the faith, was assassinated by a monk who claimed to go to him in compassion. In Korea the kings enrolled monks in their armies by thousands, in the twelfth century against the Jürtcher, in the fourteenth against the Mongols, in the sixteenth against the Japanese, and in the seventeenth against the Manchus.

CHINA

In China Fa-ch'ing led an army of 50,000 rebels in 515 C.E., and announced that any of his troops who killed an enemy would become *bodhisattvas* on the spot. Fa-ch'ing, however, was scarcely orthodox, and spoke of the Order as a gang of demons. But they were orthodox monks who were accorded military honours for their support on Tsai-tsung at the outset of the T'ang dynasty. In 619 there was an uprising of some five thousand monks who killed the sub-prefect; one of the monks, Kao T'an-cheng, actually proclaimed himself emperor with the title Mahayana. The Buddhists in general were strongly and violently opposed to the dynasty, so much so that in 621 Li Che-min deplored the disturbances which were inhibiting the spread of Buddhism. They were orthodox monks who at the end of the Sung dynasty fought against the Mongols under the banner 'Crush demons'. General Fan Tche-hiu actually formed an army of monks, called the Battalion of August Victory. Tchen-pao, a monk, was responsible for the heroic defence of Song. 'In my law', he said, 'it is a sin not to keep one's word. I promised the emperor of Song to die for him.' It was an eccentric monk who turned bandit and founded the Ming dynasty. But they were orthodox monks of the Dhyana sect in the Ming period who painted their faces blue, dyed their hair red, and with single-stick and sword repelled some Japanese pirates. And there were fringe sects, such as the White Lotus, White Cloud or Maitreya, who were military enough.

JAPAN

From the middle of the tenth century to the end of the sixteenth the Japanese monks appear to be as much soldiers as men devoted to the religious life. They quarrelled with the secular rulers; they quarrelled among themselves. The emperor Shirakawa is recorded as saying that he could not control the flooding of the river Kame or the turbulence of the monks. In the tenth century the laity (*bushi*) are found acting as police for internal order and as soldiers for external defence. Not only that, but from about 975 we find the monks themselves training as soldiers. The new policy is attributed to Ryogen, head of the Hiei-zan monastery. It looks as if there is a tendency for Buddhism to conform syncretistically with the prevailing Shinto.

The end of the tenth century saw the beginning of two centuries of internal strife between the monasteries. In the early days this was focused on the monasteries of Enryaku-ji and Onjo-ji. They operated in armies numbering several thousand, bent on arson against one another. One single campaign records the destruction of 290 religious buildings, 15 libraries, 6 belfries, 4 Shinto temples, 600 monks' dwellings, 1500 other houses, and 23,400 scrolls. By the twelfth century the focal points change to Hiei-zan and Kofuku-ji: the destruction was no less, and the marauding armies often numbered five thousand. On top of this internecine strife there were continued clashes with the government. There were occasional remonstrances – in 1114, 1151, 1156. All vain.

The next century and a half (1190–1333) is known as the epoch of Kamakura. The pattern, however, scarcely seems to mark a fresh era. The clashes between the monasteries continue interminably; so do the clashes with authority, often involving the arrest of armed monks. Not merely so, but the individual monasteries suffered from violent internal dissension; for example, in 1264 the soldier-monks of Kofuku-ji threw out their own superior. But the monasteries, riven as they were inside and out, were united on one thing – the persecution of new sects.

The Ashikaja shoguns, who were dominant in the next period, were favourable to Buddhism. This did little to alleviate the violence. There were fewer direct clashes between the monks and the secular authority, but the very favour gave the monks a footing in the corridors of political power and tempted them to engage in dynastic warfare. Meanwhile internal troubles in individual monasteries continued, the unending clashes of monastery with monastery in jealous rivalry continued, the persecution of new sects continued; Hiei-zan was particularly ruthless in its opposition to Zen.

It was only towards the end of the sixteenth century that central policy, first ruthless, then constructive, brought the situation under control. In 1571 Nobunaja destroyed the militant monastery of Hiei-zan; the mountain became a desert. The armed monks of other monasteries were put to the sword. Their roving armies were annihilated; recalcitrant centres were reduced. Hideyoshi turned to encourage peaceable, disciplined, constructive settlement. The secular power of the monks was reduced, their military power abandoned.

Zen Buddhism was introduced into Japan by Eisai in 1192. Zen involves acceptance. It is a school of contemplative mysticism, rich in paradox. By a curious historical quirk this mystical offshoot of a pacifist religion became the religion of the soldier aristocracy, and played a significant part in the formation of the Bushido ideal, the way of the militant knights or Samurai. Already by the middle of the thirteenth century Zen was a significant factor in the training of the ruling class, and the two Hojo Commissioners, Tokiyori, who was in power for a decade in mid-century, and the slightly later Tokimune, form interesting studies. Tokiyori went to a number of Zen teachers while in office, and on retirement took up the monastic life while continuing in some public service. Tokimune was an autocrat and a soldier. On one occasion he was about to take the field against a

Mongol invasion. Before setting out he went in full armour to his Zen teacher and said, 'Master, the great moment has arrived.' 'How will you go out?' asked the Master. Tokimune did not answer verbally, but gave a great roar, a leap and a pounce. 'A real lion!' said the Master. 'A fine lion's roar! March straight forward and never turn back.'

In the age of war the Samurai were in the front of the fight. They remained prominent through the period after the monasteries ceased to be fortified. There was now less fighting under the rule of the Shogun, but the Samurai, ministers of peaceful administration, continued to wear two swords and to be under military discipline. The Bushido was a moral discipline, a fleeting political and military behaviour, associated with a cult derived from Shinto, and involving a quietude and sternness of bearing derived from Zen. The Samurai were not Buddhist in thought, and the Buddhist influence upon their training, discipline and way of life is deeply ironical.

THE JUSTIFICATION OF KILLING

The main scriptural justifications for killing may be briefly summarized. In the Mahayana *Mahaparinirvana Sutra* it is told how the Buddha in one of his former lives killed some Brahmin heretics. This was done to protect the Doctrine, and to save them themselves from the consequences of continued attacks on it. When the Doctrine is in danger the Five Precepts, including the prohibition on taking life, may be ignored. So the Buddha is said to have encouraged his followers to take up arms in defence of the Order.

A second justification was that it was good to kill one in order to save two. A curious story tells of a Buddhist traveller in a caravan of five hundred. Five hundred bandits intend to attack the caravan. A scout of the bandits warns the traveller. If the Buddhist warns his fellow-travellers, they will kill the scout and suffer in hell for taking the life. If he does not the bandits will kill the travellers; more lives will be lost, and more will suffer in hell. So he kills the scout himself. The bandits consequently do not attack. Only one life is lost, and only one man, the Buddhist, suffers in hell. Another story concerns the Buddha himself killing a bandit in order to save five hundred merchants; in this story everyone goes to heaven. An additional refinement is added by the Mahayana philosopher Avenga, who said that the *bodhisattva* should wait until the mind of the other is free from evil, and then strike in a spirit of compassion and at the same time shuddering horror. In this way the *bodhisattva* actually gained merit by the act of killing.

A third justification lies in the illusory nature of existence. There is no soul, no self, nothing to kill. In one story Manjushri pretended to kill the Buddha. The Buddha congratulated Manjushri on his insight. A human being is 'merely a name, without substance, without reality, a trick of the senses, as empty as an illusion. There is no sin and no sinner. Who could be punished for having killed anyone? Between the Buddha and the sword there is non-duality.' Hui-yuan, leader of the Pure Land school, added that if Manjushri had 'actually' run the Buddha through, he would only have seemed to do wrong and would simply have been following the way.

A fourth justification comes from Asanga: it is better to kill another than to allow him to kill. A fifth claim, found in Nichiren, is that the destiny being predetermined, it can be no sin to put to death. The person killing must act either out of compassion and charity, or thoughtlessly, so that the inner peace is not disturbed; the monks of Hiei-zan when arming for war would cover their eyes.

It is a curious fact that the Theravadins with their condemnation of life have on the whole been stronger in their prohibition of killing than the Mahayana, which has found means of justifying the killer.

MODERN BUDDHISM AND WAR

In Maoist China Buddhists of radical political outlook have interpreted the Buddha's teaching so as to permit the killing of those opposed to the revolution. Thus Ming-chen wrote a long article in 1958 in which he argued that the Buddha had taken sides with the oppressed against the oppressor, and rejected the view of those who tried to eliminate all thought of class and nation as being forms of attachment. Monks were divided in their attitude to counter-revolutionaries who might take refuge among them. Some held that anything which led to the death of a living creature was wrong and that compassion demanded their protection. Others made much play with the story of Śakyamuni, while practising the way of a *bodhisattva*, killing a bandit in order to save five hundred merchants. 'Our vow not to destroy life cannot be viewed dogmatically. Killing for personal fame and profit is a breach of the vow. Killing in order to save people is in the greatest conformity with the vow.' So some monks went off to fight in Korea, being sent off in fine style by their brethren. Hsin-tao at Nanchang on 11 March 1951 actually said, 'To wipe out the American imperialist demons who are breaking world peace is, according to Buddhist doctrine, not only blameless but actually gives rise to merit.' In 1951–2 Chinese Buddhists raised money for a fighter plane which was actually called *The Chinese Buddhist*.

In Burma U Pandita, a Buddhist monk, became a leading member of the revolutionary Young Monks' Association, though subsequently striking out on his own. His vows have not prevented him from making explosives. He has remained at once a monk and a violent revolutionary, though he has recognized his own unorthodoxy; he is something of an agnostic: 'Christianity says everything depends on God; Buddhism says that everything depends on Karma. But neither can prove that this is the case.' He cites a tiger attacking a village. The Buddha says one should avoid the tiger, Marx that the village should defend itself; U Pandita sides with Marx. He still believes in Buddhist monasticism, but believes that it is even more important to fight the exploiters.

Nor is it only among the leftists that militancy is to be found. One of the most extraordinary post-war developments in Japan has been the emergence of Soka-gakkai (The Society for the Creation of Values), a lay organization of what had been a minor Nichiren sect; the membership rose in the six years 1953–9 from under a quarter of a million to over four million. The sect practises forced conversion and is generally militant.

Earlier in the century King Vajiravudh or Rama VI was crowned King of Thailand. He had been trained at Sandhurst, commissioned in the Royal Durham Light Infantry, and been given the honorary rank of general in the British army. He tried to stir up national pride and to inculcate military discipline. In 1916 the Supreme Buddhist Patriarch preached a sermon before him extolling national defence and using a text from the Buddha to defend the proposition: 'War must be prepared for even in time of peace, otherwise one would not be in time and one would be to a disadvantageous position towards one's foe.' The preface to the printed edition of this sermon asserts that it is 'an erroneous idea to suppose that the Buddha condemned all wars and people whose business it was to wage war'. What the Buddha condemned was militarism, understood as 'intolerant and unreasoning hatred, vengeance and savagery which causes men to kill from sheer blood-lust'.

MODERN BUDDHISTS AND PEACE

Present-day Buddhism has also maintained the witness to peace. In the Japanese film *Gate of Hell*, a fierce man of violence falls in love with the wife of a gentle pacifist. The lover is determined to murder the husband so as to have the woman. The wife manages to change places with her husband, so that she is herself killed by the blows intended to lead to her possession. Her sacrificial act is redemptive; the murderer becomes a monk, and there is a moving confrontation between him and the husband.

It is worth noting too the official statements by Burmese post-war leaders. The Prime Minister U Nu declared that Buddhism 'unlike the theistic creeds cannot sanction even such acts of violence as are necessary for the preservation of public order and society'. The Attorney-General, U Chan Htooa, stated: 'Buddhism is the only ideology which can give peace to the world and save it from war and destruction. . . . For that reason the peoples of the world are looking to Buddhism to save the world.' U Thant was a notably eirenic Secretary-General of the United Nations.

The Vietnam Buddhists chose a quite different way from the left-wing monks of China and Burma and consistently sought to oppose both the tyranny of the Thieu régime and the violence of the communists by non-violent means. The culmination came when a monk, Thich Quang-Duc, burnt himself to death on 11 June 1963 and others followed suit. Thich Nhat Hanh in his book *Vietnam: The Lotus in the Sea of Fire* expounded the meaning of the act. It is an extension of the act of the ordinand who burns a small spot on his body. It is a proof of the seriousness of his dedication and his measure. He is enduring the greatest sufferings to protect his people. Thich Quang-Duc's act was not suicide in the normal sense, arising from a sense of defeat and loss of hope. It was an act of construction, not of destruction. It was comparable with an action told of the Buddha in a former existence, who gave himself to a hungry lioness to save her from eating her own cubs. It was an act of compassion.

Thich Nhat Hanh himself is a poet who has expressed his non-violent philosophy in powerful verse.

> Men cannot be our enemies – even men called
>   'Vietcong!'
> If we kill men, what brothers will we have left?
> With whom shall we live then?
>
> *Condemnation*

> Even as they
> strike you down
> with a mountain of hate and violence . . .
> remember brother,
> remember
> man is not our enemy.
>
> *Recommendation*

CONCLUSION

The Buddhists were not from the first as rigid over the negative commandment as the Jains. There are stories in which the Enlightened One does not refuse meat, though he will not countenance an animal to be killed specially for him, and indeed, although there have been attempts to rationalize the story away, he is said to have died after eating a dish of boar's flesh. Similarly there is no injunction against tilling the soil, no instruction to strain or veil the indrawn breath. Still the general principles are the same. As Sariputta has it: 'What now, my brothers, is right action? To avoid killing what is alive, to avoid taking what is not given, to avoid licentiousness: this, my brothers is called right action.' It is a negative morality this far.

But there is a boundless compassion, and this is the fundamental source of the Buddha's reverence for life. He describes the tear-filled eyes of the underlings who have to round up animals for sacrifice, and forbids the monks to wear silk so that they do not have the lives of the silkworms on their conscience. In the realization that all living creatures are subject to suffering the Buddha is at one with them. The legend of his compassion grew with time.

Along with this is the internal character of the Buddhist monk.

> Now this is what you must practise well, my monks: our tempers must remain unruffled, no evil sound shall issue from our lips, we will remain friendly and sympathetic in a temper of loving-kindness, without secret malice: and we will irradiate our personality with loving feelings; from this starting-point we will . . . irradiate the whole world with broad, deep, unlimited feeling, free from anger and bitterness. This is what you must practise well, my friends.

The monk in short sends sunbeams of loving-kindness in all directions. Such a character is incompatible with violence: the righteousness of the monk is to be sympathetic and merciful, and to strive with friendly feeling for the good of all living things.

This ethical disposition is not just related to the self-fulfilment of the individual monk. According to the Enlightened One, love, kindness, loving-kindness escalate. In one story his cousin Devadatta sent a wild elephant against him, but the beast was checked in its course and brought to gentleness by the Buddha's own spirit of gentleness. There was a story the Buddha loved to tell. Brahmadatta had usurped the kingdom of Dighiti, whose name means 'suffer long'. Dighiti, living in disguise and poverty, produced a son Dighavu ('live long'). He and his wife were unmasked, denounced, and executed, but he told the son that hatred kindles hatred and can be quenched only by the refusal to hate. The boy entered the usurper's service and won his confidence. He was out hunting alone with the king, who fell asleep. Dighavu drew his sword, whirled it to strike, but recalled his father's words and stayed his hand. The king became aware of his danger in a dream, and awoke to find the sword poised. Terrified, Dighavu pleaded for pardon for his initial murderous thoughts. So the enmity was ended. 'By non-anger let anger be overcome; let evil be overcome by good; let avarice be overwhelmed by gifts; but the liar be conquered by truth; through the refusal to hatred is hatred assuaged.' The monk is a reconciler. He refuses to add to the sum of evil and the escalation of violence. He unites the estranged, rejoices in harmony, speaks words of love.

FOR FURTHER READING

BUDDHISM

Conze, E., *Buddhism*, 5th edn. Bruno Cassirer, 1974.

Demiéville, Paul, 'Le Bouddhisme et la guerre' in *Mélanges* I (Paris, Institut des Hautes Etudes Chinoises 1957), pp. 347–85.

Jun, Ohrui, 'A View of War in Buddhism' in *Tokyo University Studies 2* (1964), pp. 51–64.

Renondeau, G., 'Histoire des moines guerriers du Japon' in *Mélanges* I (Paris, Institut des Hautes Etudes Chinoises 1957), pp. 159–341.

Saddhatissa, H., *Buddhist Ethics*. Allen and Unwin, 1970.

Spiro, M. E., *Buddhism and Society*. Allen and Unwin, 1971.

Thich Nhat Hanh, *Vietnam: The Lotus in the Sea of Fire*. SCM Press, 1967.

Thich Nhat Hanh, *The Cry of Vietnam*. Santa Barbara. Unicorn Press, 1968.

Welch, Holmes, *Buddhism under Mao*. Cambridge, Mass., Harvard University Press, 1972.

Chapter 5

RELIGIONS OF THE FAR EAST

The early inhabitants of north China were agriculturalists, dependent on the processes of nature. Out of this emerged the first glimmerings of concepts later much developed, the *Tao* or way, the pattern of revolution of the heavenly bodies round the earth, of day and night, summer and winter, seedtime and harvest, the rhythm of the universe, and within this the interaction of *yang* and *yin*, the former active, male, bright, warm, procreative, the latter passive, female, dark, cold, fertile. The Shang dynasty, ruling in the second millennium B.C., honoured a legendary ancestor Shang-ti as supreme god. Their founder, Tang, established the dynasty about 1760 by violence with the approval of the divine powers. In 1122 they were in their turn ousted by the Chou dynasty, again with divine approval. The Chou called the supreme power T'ien or Heaven, and the King himself in power became T'ien Tzu, the Son of Heaven.

The most interesting member of the Chou dynasty was the so-called Duke of Chou, who intervened at a crisis, took over as regent from his nephew the King, established his power ruthlessly, then turned to conciliation, showed organizing genius, and after seven years handed the power back to his nephew. The Chou dynasty claimed to rule by the will of Heaven, and the Duke was a particularly strong exponent of the idea that history is governed by the Decree of Heaven, which the Duke calls indifferently T'ien or Shang-ti. The concept is of high importance, not least for the military side of Chinese history. Rulers claim to rule by the Decree of

Heaven; rebels and usurpers claim to replace them by the Decree of Heaven.

The other important aspect of early religion in China is ancestor-worship, which was universally practised, the ancestors being always consulted before any major undertaking.

K'UNG

K'ung, known as the Master, K'ung Fu Tzu, in the West Confucius, was born in 551 B.C. in the small state of Lu in Shantung, 'without rank and in humble circumstances'. He had a good education; it gave him a career as a minor official; and he saw education as the key to changing the world. He was himself a sound administrator, without conspicuous genius, and without success in introducing reforms. He set up as a teacher of ceremonial (*li*), and of administrative and political skills. He died in 479. His ideas lived on, and may most conveniently be studied in *The Analects*, a collection made some seventy years later. His thought moulded Chinese social and political history for 2400 years, until the coming of the Communists.

K'ung was not in the obvious sense a religious thinker or prophet. But the way (*Tao*) that he taught was not just the way of man but the way of Heaven (T'ien). 'If it is the will of Heaven that the way shall prevail, then the way will prevail' (*Analects* 14, 38). But although he speaks of the Will of Heaven, he does not think in terms of a personal god, still less in terms of mystical vision. It is rather that he sees life *sub specie aeternitatis*, and lifts it above the mere relativities of an immediate situation. It was characteristic of him to rebuke otherworldly piety: 'You have not learned how to serve men; how can you serve spirits?' 'You do not understand life; how can you understand death?' But he believed that his own mission was by will of Heaven, and when faced with misunderstanding comforted himself with the thought 'Heaven understands me!'

K'ung's thought in fact appears as a kind of ethical humanism. It is directed to *li*, propriety in all the relationships of life, motivated by *jen*, a spirit of loving-kindness. Basic to this is the principle of reciprocity, not to do to others things you would not wish done to yourself. They said of him that he taught four things – literature, personal conduct, being one's true self, and honesty. It was, in the strict sense, a conventional social ethic. It was not revolutionary in the obvious sense. But it brought the gentlemen of the aristocracy up against standards of conduct, and asserted that those who practised those standards were gentlemen, whatever their birth.

K'ung similarly was no pacifist. *The Annals*, which he may have edited in old age, contain a factual but not disapproving account of military campaigns and primitive expeditions. The upper classes of his day formed a military élite; K'ung's gentleman (*chün tzu*) was originally a knight trained for war. He was not out to challenge that. He accepted vengeance and the blood feud as manly duties; he believed that the values of society must be defended by violence against those who knew no other argument. But war must be a last resort and subject to the principles of justice. He put this with characteristic pragmatism; an army's morale would be reduced at all levels unless officers and privates alike were convinced that they had justice on their side. He stressed education, not merely in the techniques of warfare, but in understanding the cause for which one is fighting. 'To lead a people who have not been educated in war, is to throw them away.' At the same time he believed that the power of justice could transform a seemingly weaker army. 'If I feel in my heart that I am wrong, I must stand in fear even though my opponent is the least formidable of men. But if my own heart tells me that I am right, I shall go forward even against thousands and ten thousands.'

K'ung thus did not challenge war; he refined it, but that refinement itself proved a challenge. For a check on unrestricted war proved to be a check on war, and as Max Weber put it, 'With the rule of the literati the increasingly pacifist turn of ideologies was natural and vice versa.'

TAO-TE-CHING

Tao-te-ching (*The Way-Power Book*) is attributed to a shadowy figure called Lao-tzu, an older contemporary of K'ung, who thought him as mysterious and ineluctable as a dragon, and who was charged by him with being obsequious and ambitious. Some scholars think that there was no such person; certainly we know little enough about him.

But we have the book. The right life is one in accord or harmony with the Tao. He who follows the Tao has *te*, power or virtue. But how to find and follow the Tao? Through *wu-wei*, non-effort, not striving, receptivity. 'The highest excellence is like water. Because the excellence of water lies in benefiting all things without striving against them, and in settling in the lowest place which no one wants to take, it comes close to the Tao' (8).

It follows for a number of reasons that mystical Taoism places its weight in the scale of pacifism. In the first place, Lao-tzu opposes ambition, political power, worldly authority; these are the products of striving. He who delights in slaughter is no use as a ruler (31). In the second place the Taoists hold to something like an anarchist philosophy of government: the less the better (17). The more laws, the more law-breakers. Capital punishment is not so much immoral as futile; a person whose life is lived face to face with death will not fear the death penalty, and no one is qualified to pronounce it on another. Weapons are instruments of evil (31). Only when a people have fallen away from the Tao are war horses found on the frontiers; when Tao prevails the horses are dunging the fields (46). Anyone who serves the government with Tao does not dominate the world by violence (30). Thirdly, there is a strong element of pragmatism buttressing the high principle of *wu-wei*, and an awareness, for example, of the escalation of violence, and of the destructive power of war. 'The use of force usually brings requital. Wherever armies are stationed, briars and thorns grow. Great wars are always followed by famines' (30). Violent people do not die a natural death (42). Fourthly, there is a strong element of compassion, especially for the suffering of the common people. 'For the slaughter of the multitude, let us weep with sorrow and grief. For a victory, let us observe the occasion with funeral ceremonies' (31). Fifthly, behind this is a sense of the relativity of earthly judgements. For if all is of the Tao then all is part of the all-embracing harmony of the universe. We cannot ever say that we are right to the exclusion of other views. The pattern of the world is compounded of opposites (2). Sixthly, there is a philosophy of victory through suffering. 'To yield is to be preserved whole. To be bent is to become straight' (22). One saying, though the meaning is a shade uncertain, seems to run 'When two armies face one another victory lies with the man of sorrows' (or possibly 'the one which yields') (69). Finally there is a distinct sense that peace is the natural state of mankind, and if people would not interfere, and would let Tao have its way, the world would be at peace of its own accord (37).

It is interesting to reflect that according to a story traceable back to the second century C.E. Lao-tzu, his work in China completed, travelled to the West and appeared in India as the Buddha.

MO TI

A third great initiative towards a social philosophy was taken in the fifth century by Mo Ti (*c.* 480–390 B.C.). We know little enough about him. He was associated with the small state of Sung, which tended to be a buffer-state between larger military powers. He was brought up in the school of K'ung, but came to feel that Confucianism as he knew it did not have the answer to social and political evil. His own philosophy had a religious dimension in much the same way as that of K'ung, and spoke of the Tao in much the same way. What he questioned was the Confucians' use of precedents and fixed rules.

Mo Ti's positive philosophy was based on love (*ai*), universal love. Love which was limited in its range was divisive. Love which was confined to members of one's own family, clan or state led to nepotism, jealousy and war. If everyone looked on the property of others as if it were his own, there would be no theft. Universal love would end all the contentions and troubles of the world. He defended his teaching both in absolute principle and on grounds of expediency. Mo Ti has been called a Utilitarian, and indeed declared that he could not advocate anything which was not useful. But he is essentially of those who say that if an action is good it must in the end be useful, not of those who start from utility and use it to define goodness. This is a religious stance, a doctrine of the Tao.

Mo Ti was a relentless opponent of war. Perhaps because of the sufferings of his own state of Sung, he had a direct awareness of the evils of war. He was not a pacifist; on the contrary he trained a dedicated company of his disciples in defensive warfare. Aggressive warfare was ruled out. Much of Mo Ti's argument against war was utilitarian. He argued that war was not profitable. If you fight in winter it is too cold, in summer too hot, in spring or autumn it takes the workers away from agriculture. If you fight at any time you lose weapons and tents and transport and horses and oxen and human lives. But, they said, look at the four states which have grown powerful by war. Well, he answered, what of the ten thousand which have gone under? Would you call useful a medicine which cured four patients out of ten thousand? This argument would hardly persuade those in power, and he argued further that the attack on a small state by a large state in fact injured both, and that injustice never paid. War is destructive; conquered territories are devastated; conquerors are no better than kleptomaniacs. Justice and virtue alone, not the sword, could conquer the world.

But Mo Ti was prepared to fight, and was a defensive strategist. One famous story tells how he went to the ruler of Ch'u when he was about to attack Sung, and invited him to discuss the assault and defence. Every plan of attack produced was countered. There was one left. Mo Ti knew what it was – to murder him. But he had three hundred trained followers on the walls who could operate without him. The attack was called off.

All this seems to have little to do with religion. But the real force of Mo Ti's rejection of war lay in his doctrine of universal love. If everyone in the world would practise universal love, then the whole world would enjoy peace and order. Mo Ti did not in fact believe that men naturally love one another, and appealed to arguments which established the will of Heaven or God. So that in another saying he declared that obedience to the will of Heaven would bring peace and order.

PACIFISM IN THE FIFTH CENTURY

Out of this mesh of the Confucian moral critique of war, the Taoist doctrine of *wu-wei* and Mo Ti's active concern for peace emerged peace propaganda. The *Chuang-Tzu* records pacifists as early as the fifth century B.C.

They sought to unite men through an ardent love in universal brotherhood. To fight against lusts and evil desires was their chief endeavour. When they were reviled, they did not consider it a shame: they were intent on nothing but the redemption of men from quarrelling. They forbade aggression, and preached disarmament in order to redeem mankind from war. This teaching they carried throughout the world. They admonished princes and instructed subjects. The world was not ready to accept their teaching, but they held to it all the more firmly. It was said that high and low tried to avoid meeting them, but that they forced themselves on people.

This was a high missionary endeavour for peace. We must however remember that it would be meaningless except against the background of continual wars and fighting.

MENG TZU (MENCIUS)

In Meng Tzu (372–298 B.C.) we can see K'ung's ethic of human love extended to all living creatures. A good story tells how King Suan of Tsi had compassion on an ox which was dedicated for sacrifice, and had it released. Meng Tzu commented that such an attitude was appropriate to a king of the world. The love of war was his chief charge against the rulers. He assailed successful generals as criminals. Those who make fighting their profession should be liable to severe punishment, and alongside them those who direct their power to aggression. 'When land is the cause of contention, corpses fill the field; when a city is the cause of contention, corpses fill the circuit of the walls. This is teaching the very soil beneath us to devour human flesh – a crime for which death cannot atone.' But where Mo Ti insisted that war was unprofitable and made his appeal on those grounds Meng Tzu refused to use the argument and based his appeal to rules on loving-kindness (*jen*) and righteousness (*i*). Underlying this was his belief in the fundamental goodness of human nature. From this came also his advocacy of democracy on religious grounds. 'Heaven sees as the people see, and Heaven hears as the people hear.' 'The people rank highest in a state, the spirits of the Land and Grain come next, and the ruler is of the least account.'

INTELLECTUAL DEVELOPMENTS

By now the main patterns of religious thought as applied to society had taken shape. In the centuries which followed there were developments in the main schools. Chuang Tzu for example developed the thought of *Tao-te-ching*. He identifies the Tao with non-being, and vigorously insists that the only way to govern is through non-government. 'Everything in the world longs for peace. Why then should there be some who address themselves so earnestly to governing empires?' Chuang Tzu stresses the relativism inherent in the doctrines of the Tao, and directs it to political doctrines of equality rather than privilege and freedom rather than constraint.

Among the Confucians Hsün Tzu was perhaps the most interesting. He held, against Meng Tzu, that men are evil by nature; he held a corresponding doctrine of the necessity of government, of a ruling class, and of wise rulers. One important aspect of Hsün's thought was the separation of religion from philosophy. He himself was an agnostic, and he claimed that man depended upon himself, not upon Heaven, for his salvation.

THE DIALECTICIANS

Hui Shih perhaps lived in the fourth century B.C., a native of the state of Sung. He belonged to a philosophical group known as the Dialecticians or the School of Forms and Names, and in a period of war preached universal love and pacifism. He is recorded as saying, 'Love all things equally; the universe is one' (*Chuang Tzu* 33). It may have been this egalitarianism which led him to his doctrine of 'the abolition of honourable position' (*Lü-shih Ch'un Ch'iu* 21.5), though unfortunately we do not know how he applied this in detail. We find him also, in a phrase which makes a pun in the original, advocating a cessation of hostility between the states of Ch'i and Ch'u (*Han-fei-tzu* 30). Hui Shih was noted for his paradoxes, logical and mystical; he does not seem to have belonged to the Mohist or pacifist school of thought.

So too in the following century we find another of the leading Dialecticians, Kung-sun Lung, a native of Chao, advocating pacifism on the rulers of Chao and Yen, again in the name of universal love: 'The idea in ending war springs out of a mind holding universal love towards the world' (*Lü-shih Ch'un Ch'iu* 18.1) Kung-sun Lung was preoccupied with a kind of Platonic Theory of Forms. Again we sense a general pacifism in the philosophic climate.

It is interesting to notice that the later Mohists accepted the logical tools of the Dialecticians in defence of their doctrine of universal love.

THE LEGALISTS

The philosophy of Legalism was a philosophy of counter-revolution and a fresh assertion of authority. The Legalists stood against the democratic and pacifistic trends in the religious philosophies of the time. Against the idea that the rule exists for the sake of the people they proclaimed the rights of the ruler. Against the pacifism of Mo Ti they asserted the glory of war. They are found advising monarchs how to increase their military power. The Confucians claimed that political power depended on conquest, which depended on economic resources and a disciplined army. So the Legalist advisers punished dissension with death, set up a system of informers, rewarded military valour and excluded from the victory-class any who did not show it, and established a rigid class structure.

FROM HAN TO SUNG

Legalism became a dead letter before the end of the third century B.C., and under the Han dynasty Confucianism became more and more influential. But the new Confucianism had a strong eclectic element, and, for example, the emperor Wu in the second century B.C. could graft on to it a glorification of war as vigorous as any Legalist's.

Two other important factors helped to modify the picture of an intertwining of developed traditions. The first was the coming of Buddhism. The exact story of this is not easy to trace, but Buddhism had reached China by the Christian era, and by 381 C.E. it is said that nine-tenths of the people of north-west China were Buddhists. The advent of Buddhism supported the life-regarding, peace-abiding side of Chinese religious thought. At the same time Buddhism itself was liable to compromise and take on the social customs of the community into which it was penetrating.

Alongside this were changes in Taoism. From being a high religious philosophy for the few it became a popular cult for the many. The advent of Buddhism encouraged the Taoists to develop still further a rival system of temples, liturgy and monasteries. One curious episode relates to the organizers of a Taoist health cult in Szechuan in the middle of the second century C.E. Two warlords, Chang Lu and Chang Hsiu, joined to foster the cult, whose priests were army officers and whose converts were called 'demon soldiers'. So far had the Taoists moved from *wu-wei* that in 184 C.E. they organized a great public uprising in Shantung against oppressive social conditions. The Yellow Turbans combined an evangelical religious movement involving communal life and public confession of sins, with military and political revolution. They took up arms and secured control of a large section of the country, at the cost of half a million lives. The suppression of this religious revolt led to a civil war which, in Balazs's words, changed China 'from a powerful empire into one vast cemetery'.

China was reunited by the T'ang dynasty, and this period and the following Sung dynasty saw the restoration of Confucian influence.

THE BOOK OF ACTIONS AND REWARDS

Something of reverence for life is found in the *Kan-Ying-P'ien* (*The Book of Actions and Rewards*). This dates from the Sung Dynasty (960–1280 C.E.) and comprises some 212 pithy ethical maxims. These include 'Have a pitiful heart for all creatures' and 'One must bring no sorrow even on worms, plants and trees'. There is condemnation of those who shoot and hunt, disturb nests or burrows. Insects are not to be trodden underfoot or destroyed by boiling water. Even grass and flowers are not to be picked without reason. There is sound practical advice: 'Do not allow your children to amuse themselves by playing with flies or butterflies or little birds. It is not merely that such proceedings may result in damage to living creatures: they waken in young hearts the inclination to cruelty and murder.' There is a positive as well as a negative side to this, a clear command to help any living creature in need. The nature behind this is to accord with the impartial kindness of heaven and earth; a Christian reader thinks immediately of a similar passage in the N.T. (Matt. 5.45).

Three delightful stories illustrate these principles. In the first a woman suffering from tuberculosis had the brains of a hundred sparrows prescribed as a medicine. She saw the victims and said, 'Shall it happen that a hundred living creatures are killed to cure me? I would rather die than let them suffer so!' She let the birds go free – and was miraculously cured. The second was a story of Tsao-Pin, whose house was falling apart. His children wanted to repair it, but he saw that the cracks allowed numerous living creatures to escape from the winter's cold. In the third story Wu-Tang, a hunter, came on a stag and fawn playing. He shot the fawn, and when the stag returned to tend it, pitifully, shot him too. Then he saw another stag, shot another arrow, misfired and struck his own son. As he burst into tears he heard a voice: 'Tang, the stag loved its fawn just as much as you loved your son.'

The *Kan-Ying-P'ien* undoubtedly has elements derived from Indian thought. But this approach and these stories seem purely Chinese. Buddhism fostered and nurtured it, but did not create it.

THE MODERN ERA IN CHINA

The later centuries saw western interference in the affairs of China. This had cataclysmic historical results, but there has been in religion and thought generally a preference for maintaining indigenous traditions. Yen Fu (1854–1921), who did more than anyone else to introduce western thought into China, in the end rejected it with significant words: 'It seems to me that in three centuries of progress the peoples of the west have achieved four principles: to be selfish, to kill others, to have little integrity, and to feel little shame. How different are the principles of Confucius and Mencius, as broad and deep as Heaven and Earth, designed to benefit all men everywhere.'

So Confucian principles remained and still remain strong, and even the Communists have been divided as to whether they are to be rejected as a straitjacket preventing change and destroying the human spirit, or embraced as part of the distinctive traditions of China.

So the father of the Chinese Republic, Sun Yat-sen, a military revolutionary, could declare in 1912 that the Chinese people were 'continuing the historic struggle of the French and American peoples for republican institutions'. But later he declared, 'What we need to learn from Europe is science, not political philosophy. As for the true principles of political philosophy, the Europeans need to learn them from China.' Characteristically he described saving mankind from injustice as his 'Heaven-appointed task'.

Right into the twentieth century Taoism carried reverence for life among its central tenets. In three hundred commandments laid on Taoist monks, the first was 'Thou shalt kill no living thing, or damage its life', the second 'Thou shalt not eat the flesh and blood of any living thing'. The great commandments of the *Kan-Ying-P'ien* are also incorporated. Taoism has also retained many elements which seem superstitious. For this reason it has come under attack. It lacks leadership and organization. But it is very deeply rooted in Chinese tradition, and may in the long run prove more resistant than Confucianism or Buddhism.

With the Communist revolution Maoism has become the dominant philosophy of China. As a philosophy it is non-religious and indeed anti-religious, but, as Ninian Smart has shown, it has many features which are also found in religion; I. C. K. Yang has called Chinese Communism 'a non-theistic faith'. Mao was an advocate and practitioner of revolutionary violence, as in his celebrated dictum that 'political power grows out of the barrel of a gun'. He saw war as the continuation of politics, the highest form of struggle for resolving contradictions. Without armed struggle the revolution could not triumph. Wars are divided into two kinds, just and unjust. 'All wars that are progressive are just, and all wars that impede progress are unjust.' Revolutionary war is an antitoxin eliminating the enemy's poison and at the same time purging the revolutionary party. The ultimate aim is the abolition of war, 'but war can be abolished only through war'. Mao calls war 'a monster of mutual slaughter among men', and believes that it can and will be eliminated, but only by opposing war with war.

JAPANESE SHINTO

Shinto, the traditional religion of Japan, became one of the most militaristic of religions. The name is derived from Chinese, Shen-tao, the Way of the Gods, in Japanese Kami-no-michi. Its origins are obscure. In its earlier form it seems to have been primarily concerned with fertility and, associated with this, cleansing from pollution. Shinto is rich in mythology. From the primeval chaos emerged three divine powers, the Divine Land of the Centre of Creation, the Venerable Creator on High, and the Divine Venerable Creator. In the seventh generation appeared the brother and sister Izanagi and Izanami, He-who-invites and She-who-invites; they gave birth to eighty lands, eighty islands and eight million gods, notably Amaterasu, the sun-goddess, and Susanowo, the storm-god, the power of violence. The imperial ruler of Japan, the Son of Heaven, was believed to be descended from Amaterasu, and was himself regarded as divine until the Emperor Hirohito renounced that divinity in 1946.

The essence of Shinto as a religion lies in activity. Life is a striving, and he who refrains from progressive action in search of static divinity belies his own divine nature. The divine is to be formed in the kami, the spirits, spirits of growth, of nature, and of the ancestors. In the eighth-century *Chronicle of Japan (Nihon-gi)* is written 'The God who originally founded this country is the god who descended from Heaven and established this state in the period when Heaven and Earth became separated, and when the trees and herbs had speech.' Deep within Shinto there is a drive to action and expansion and striving (the diametrical opposite of philosophical Taoism), and a solidarity with the land and the people. Further, while Shinto in one aspect stressed submission, in another it was militant. Swords, spears, bows and arrows were symbols of deities, if not themselves divine. Susanowo presented Amaterasu with a sword, which Prince Yamato-takem used on his expeditions, and which became one of the imperial insignia. Other fighting gods include Futsu-nushi (Sharp-cutting Lord) and Take-mika-zuchi (Valiant-august-thunder). Shinto in fact at this stage was a typical tribal religion; militancy in the community and communal cults grew hand-in-hand.

In Shinto family worship, the local communal cult and the state cult all play their part, and state Shinto became the focal point of religious patriotism. By an imperial rescript of 1868 followed by another in 1870, Shinto became the established state religion.

The Grand Imperial Shrine of Ise, the Dai Jingu, was the place where the regalia of the imperial dynasty were kept. It was here that after the Russo-Japanese war Admiral Togo made his pilgrimage of thanksgiving. There was in fact a curious anomaly in the nineteenth century, as Buddhism, Christianity, and shrine Shinto became recognized and accepted religions. State Shinto was seen as separate from all of them; it was taught in all schools; it was scarcely considered as a religion at all, and obligatory on practitioners of all religions. There was some attempt to eliminate the word Shinto from all public pronouncements: in 1872 it was called Dai-kyo (Great Teaching), inculcating three tenets:

1 The principles of reverence for the Deities and of patriotism shall be observed.
2 The heavenly Reason and the way of Humanity shall be promulgated.
3 The Throne shall be revered and the authorities obeyed.

It was in fact a focal point for militant nationalism. In actual fact however there was no religious distinction between the state shrines and the local shrines, and the obligation to observe state Shinto involved worshippers of all religions in the local Shinto observances.

From this arose a sense of Japan's benevolent destiny ordained by the gods. Japan was to be the saviour of the world. Japan's wars became holy wars. The watchword of imperial policy was 'The Whole World under One Roof': the religious instrument of this was the Imperial Army. When Japan joined with Nazi Germany in 1940 the express purpose of the alliance at the Japanese end was said to be 'to enhance justice on earth and make of the world one household'.

With the end of the Second World War the state Shinto shrines, three hundred in number, were disestablished, and the teaching of Shinto in schools was abolished. The vacuum encouraged the development of numbers of independent Shinto sects, some of which had existed from the previous century. On the whole these sects have had little political implication, but one, the Konko-kyo sect established by Bunjiro, holds to a belief in One God who is perfect Goodness, and who calls his followers to universal brotherhood.

In Shinto we thus have had the experience of a nature-cult, with many gods, local festivals, an elaborate ritual and priesthood, a strong family-feeling and ancestor-worship, and very little impact on public life. We have had the most militaristic of religions, a kind of religious nationalism. And we have had an ethical monotheism proclaiming universal brotherhood.

The other great religion of Japan, as of China, has been Buddhism. This of course has also interacted with and modified Shinto, and been modified in its turn; certainly the real inspiration of the Samurai, however much Zen Buddhism touched on their art of swordsmanship, was Shinto, and in the Samurai we see Buddhism almost at the service of Shinto.

Confucianism was particularly influential in Japan in the seventeenth century. Yamaga Soko (1622–85) in particular brought Confucianism to bear on the life of the Samurai and the Bushido ideal. Human life is the expression of cosmic life in social order. This must be backed by education directed towards magnanimity and courage. The life of the Samurai is the application of these qualities in government and war, and military training should be a combination of ethics and strategy. Soko gave lectures under the title *Shinto*. The contents show the scope of his thinking and the nature of his emphasis:

1 The fundamental principles: fidelity to vocation; and earnest desire to carry out the way; effort to that end.
2 Training of the mind: composure; magnanimity; purity; gentleness; refinement, etc.
3 Training in virtues and perfection of ability.
4 Introspection and self-discipline.
5 Dignity and propriety.
6 Vigilance in daily life.

It is an unexpected course in military science, and again we are seeing Confucianism at the service of Shinto. Soko was suspect as a private individual with a mastery of military science, but he was highly influential.

FOR FURTHER READING

Anesaki, M., *History of Japanese Religion*, 2nd edn. Routledge, 1963.

Chan, W.-T., *The Way of Lao Tzu*. Indianapolis, Bobbs-Merrill, 1963.

Creel, H. G., *Chinese Thought*. Methuen, 1962.

Creemers, W. H. M., *Shrine Shinto after World War II*. Leiden, Brill, 1968.

Fung Yu-Lain, *A History of Chinese Philosophy*, Eng. tr. Peiping, Vetch, 1937.

Herbert, J., *Shinto at the Fountain Head of Japan*. Allen and Unwin, 1967.

Holtom, D. C., *The National Faith of Japan: A Study in Modern Shinto*. Kegan Paul, 1938.

Holtom, D. C., *Modern Japan and Shinto Nationalism*, 2nd edn. Chicago, Paragon, 1947.

Kitegawa, J. M., *Religion in Japanese History*. New York, Columbia University Press, 1966.

Mao Tse-Tung, *Quotations from Chairman Mao Tse-Tung*. Peking, Foreign Languages Press, 1966.

Mason, J. W. T., *The Meaning of Shinto*, 2nd edn. Port Washington, Kennikat, 1967.

Maspero, J. H., *Le Taoisme et les religions chinoises*. Paris, Gallimard, 1971.

Ono, S., *Shinto: The Kami Way*. Tokyo, Bridgeway, 1962.

Ross, F. H., *Shinto: The Way of Japan*. Boston, Beacon Press, 1965.

Smart, N., *Mao*, Penguin, 1975.

Smith, D. H., *Chinese Religions*. Weidenfeld, 1968.

Smith, D. H., *Confucius*. Temple Smith, 1973.

Waley, A., *The Way and Its Power*. Allen and Unwin, 1934.

Weber, Max, *The Religions of China*, Eng. tr. Glencoe, Free Press, 1951.

Yang, C. K., *Religion in Chinese Society*. Berkeley and Los Angeles, University of California Press, 1961.

Chapter 6

JUDAISM

THE PEOPLE OF THE LORD

If we were required to put a historical date to the beginning of Judaism we should see it in the deliverance of the Israelites from Egypt under the leadership of Moses, and the subsequent covenant at Mt Sinai. It is one of the constant praises of the Lord that he brought his people up from Egypt (e.g. Ps. 78.12; 80.8; 81.10; etc.). This was a military deliverance.

> The Lord is a warrior: the Lord is his name.
> The chariots of Pharaoh and his army
> he has cast into the sea;
> the flower of his officers
> are engulfed in the Red Sea.
> The watery abyss has covered them,
> they sank in the depths like a stone.
> Thy right hand, O Lord, is majestic in strength:
> thy right hand, O Lord, shattered the enemy.
>
> Exod. 15.3–6

So with the entry into Canaan. Joshua puts an extended historical narrative into the mouth of the Lord. He records the deliverance from Egypt and goes on:

> Then I brought you into the land of the Amorites who lived east of the Jordan; they fought against you, but I delivered them into your hands; you took possession of their country and I destroyed

them for your sake. The King of Moab, Balak son of Zippor, took the field against Israel. He sent for Balaam son of Beor to lay a curse on you, but I would not listen to him. Instead of that he blessed you; and so I saved you from the power of Balak. Then you crossed the Jordan and came to Jericho. The citizens of Jericho fought against you, but I delivered them into your hands. I spread panic before you, and it was this, not your sword or your bow, that drove out the two kings of the Amorites. I gave you land on which you had not laboured, cities which you had never built; you have lived in those cities and you eat the produce of vineyards and olive-groves which you did not plant.

Josh. 24.8–13

The historical books of the Bible are full of such battles, and the Ark of the Lord represents the very presence of God in the campaign (1 Sam. 4.1–11).

The Israelites were a military people; in this regard they were a people of their time. They believed in the all-mighty power of God. All that happened happened by his will. If Pharaoh's heart was hardened, God hardened it; if God had not hardened it, it could not have been hardened. If Israel conquered in battle it was through the will and power of the Lord. So he is 'the Lord, mighty in battle' (Ps. 24–8). He is the Lord of Hosts. David goes out against Goliath 'in the name of the Lord of Hosts, the God of the army of Israel which you have defied' (1 Sam. 17.45). Hezekiah says of Sennacherib, 'He has human strength; but we have the Lord our God to help us and to fight our battles' (2 Chron. 32.8). In the Book of the Law it is written that before battle the priest shall say, 'Hear, O Israel, this day you are joining battle with the enemy; do not lose heart or be afraid, or give way to panic in face of them; for the Lord your God will go with you to fight your enemy for you and give you the victory' (Deut. 20.3–4). So Nehemiah restores the walls of Jerusalem, with half the men building and half standing to arms, and himself keeping hold of his sword, and tells his people, 'Wherever the trumpet sounds, rally to us there and God will fight for us' (Neh. 4.16–23). So Judas Maccabaeus, facing the Greek armies, exhorts his men, 'Do not be afraid of their great numbers or panic when they charge. Remember

79

how our fathers were saved at the Red Sea, when Pharaoh and his army were pursuing them. Let us cry now to Heaven to favour our cause, to remember the covenant made with our fathers, and to crush this army before us today. Then all the Gentiles will know that there is One who saves and liberates Israel' (1 Macc. 4.8–11).

But in other ways the Israelites differed from the peoples round about. In the first place they were linked to Yahweh, the Lord, by a covenant. He was not a mere projection of their being on to the infinite. He was independent of them. Chemosh was god of Moab. If Moab ceased to exist, apparently Chemosh ceased to exist. If Moab was defeated, Chemosh was defeated. But the God of Israel was not in that way indissolubly linked with Israel. If Israel ceased to exist, he did not cease to exist, for his relation to Israel was covenanted, not organic. If Israel was defeated, that was due to the Lord's withdrawal of support; he was not defeated. This further meant that what he was to Israel he could be to all people. The covenant bore within it the seeds of universalism. So Amos proclaims the judgement of the Lord on Moab for atrocities committed not against Israel but against Edom (Amos 2.1–3), and cries:

> Are not you Israelites like Cushites to me?
>   says the Lord.
> Did I not bring Israel up from Egypt,
> the Philistines from Caphtor, the Aramaeans from Kir?
>
> Amos 9.7

So
> In days to come
> the mountain of the Lord's house
> shall be set over all other mountains,
>   lifted high above the hills.
> All the nations shall come streaming to it.
>
> Isa. 2.2

The second difference was that the covenant was associated with a moral code, simple but exalted, the Ten Commandments. From the first the Lord made moral demands of his people, and as the prophets interpreted the word of the Lord to his people those moral claims became more profound and more demanding. So while the way of violence exists, it stands under judgement.

In Genesis 34 the story is told of the way Shechem outraged Jacob's daugher Dinah. Two of Jacob's sons, Simeon and Levi, used treacherous violence to avenge her honour. Years later, as he died, Jacob cursed them:

> Simeon and Levi are brothers,
> their spades became weapons of violence.
> My soul shall not enter their council,
> my heart shall not join their company;
> for in their anger they killed men,
> wantonly they hamstrung oxen.
> A curse be on their anger because it was fierce;
> a curse on their wrath because it was ruthless!
> I will scatter them in Jacob,
> I will disperse them in Israel.

Gen. 49.5–7

Again, David is in many ways the heroic soldier-king, despite the corrupting effects of power which led, for example, to the elimination of Uriah so that the king could enjoy his wife. He hoped as the culmination of his career to 'build a house as a resting-place for the Ark of the Covenant of the Lord which might serve as a footstool for the feet of our God'. He made preparations to build it. But God said to him, 'You shall not build a house in honour of my name, for you have been a fighting man and you have shed blood' (1 Chron. 28.2–3). The prohibition here arises not from his unjust acts, but precisely from the fact that he has been a soldier. The far less admirable and attractive Solomon, ruler of a heavily armed state, but not himself a front-line fighter, is granted the privilege.

A third example: Jehu, with Elisha behind him, massacres the apostate house of Ahab and the Baal-worshippers (2 Kings 9–10). But the prophet Hosea sees these same actions as a crime.

Call him Jezreel, for in a little while I will punish the line of Jehu for the blood shed in Jezreel and put an end to the kingdom of Israel.

Hos. 1.4

Alongside the military fervour there developed a rich compassion. It is notable at the end of the book of Jonah. Jonah has denounced

Nineveh, and proclaimed its destruction. The people repent and the Lord withholds the threatened disaster, for he is 'a god compassionate and gracious, long-suffering, ever constant and true, maintaining constancy to thousands, forgiving iniquity, rebellion, and sin, and not sweeping the guilty clean away' (Exod. 34.6). Jonah is displeased, but the Lord says, 'Should not I be sorry for the great city of Nineveh, with its hundred and twenty thousand who cannot tell their right hand from their left, and cattle without number?' (Jon. 4.11).

Two excellent stories of compassion come in the historical books. One has to do with Elisha, who did not always show compassion. The Aramaeans were trying to capture Elisha. They were deluded and led into Samaria. The King of Israel cried excitedly, 'My father, shall I smite them? Shall I smite them?' But Elisha told him to let them eat and drink and return to their master. 'And Aramaean raids on Israel ceased' (2 Kings 6.8–23). The other is perhaps a remote source of the parable of the Good Samaritan. The northern kingdom of Israel had commited an act of aggression against the southern kingdom of Judah, and taken a large number of prisoners. A Samaritan prophet named Oded went out to meet the army and insisted on the return of the prisoners of war. 'They clothed them and shod them, gave them food and drink, and anointed them; those who were tottering from exhaustion they conveyed on the backs of asses' (2 Chron. 28.1–15).

There is a strong biblical tradition that the people of God should rely on him rather than on military power.

> Some boast of chariots and some of horses,
> but our boast is the name of the Lord our God.
> They totter and fall,
> but we rise up and are full of courage.

Ps. 20.7–8

> A King is not saved by a great army,
> nor a warrior delivered by great strength.
> A man cannot trust his horse to save him,
> nor can it deliver him for all its strength.
> The Lord's eyes are turned towards those who fear him.

Ps. 33.16–18

JUDAISM

The Lord sets no store by the strength of a horse
and takes no pleasure in a runner's legs;
his pleasure is in those who fear him,
who wait for his true love.

Ps. 147.10–11

These are the words of the Lord God the Holy One of Israel;
Come back, keep peace, and you will be safe;
in stillness and in staying quiet, there lies your strength.
But you would have none of it; you said, No,
we will take horse and flee;
therefore you shall be put to flight:
We will ride apace;
therefore swift shall be the pace of your pursuers.

Isa. 30.15–16

The classic example of the Lord's action is the destruction of Sennacherib's army (2 Kings 19.1–36; 2 Chron. 32.1–23; Isa. 37.1–38). Here there was deliverance, but a violent deliverance. But a century later Jeremiah proclaimed the will of the Lord that Nebuchadnezzar should be a world-ruler, and that Judah should submit to him. The alternative was destruction. 'Serve the king of Babylon and save your lives. Why should this city become a ruin?' (Jer. 27.17). It might seem a matter of pragmatic calculation, but Jeremiah proclaims it as religious obedience. In general we can trace the view put by Zechariah. 'Not by might, nor by power, but by my Spirit, says the Lord of hosts' (Zech. 4.6).

SHALOM

There is a strong biblical tradition also that the Lord is a god who puts an end to war.

From end to end of the earth he stamps out war:
he breaks the bow, he snaps the spear
and burns the shield in the fire.

Ps. 46.9

I will break bow and sword and weapon of war and sweep them off
the earth, so that all living creatures may lie down without fear.

Hos. 2.18

> They shall beat their swords into mattocks
> and their spears into pruning-knives;
> nation shall not lift sword against nation
> nor ever again be trained for war.

Isa. 2.4 = Mic. 4.3

This last is a direct negation of the opposite injunction found in Joel
(3.10).

There is in fact a commitment to peace. The word for peace is
shalom. It does not just mean the absence of war: Jeremiah
fulminates against those who cry 'Peace! Peace!' where there is no
peace. It comes from a root meaning 'wholeness'; it indicates a total
condition of well-being. So Micah spells out the state where the
swords are beaten into mattocks: 'each man shall dwell under his
own vine, under his own fig-tree, undisturbed' (Mic. 4.4). The
exaltation of peace runs through the Scriptures. Hear the psalmist
who calls on his people to 'turn from evil and do good, seek peace
and pursue it' (Ps. 34.14).

> Let me hear the words of the Lord:
> are they not words of peace,
>> peace to his people and his loyal servants
>> and to all who turn and trust in him?
>
> Deliverance is near to those who worship him,
>> so that glory may dwell in our land.
> Love and fidelity have come together;
> justice and peace join hands.

Ps 85.8–10

> Pray for the peace of Jerusalem:
>> 'May those who love you prosper;
> peace be within your ramparts
>> and prosperity in your palaces.'

> For the sake of these my brothers and my friends,
> > I will say, 'Peace be within you.'
> For the sake of the house of the Lord our God
> > I will pray for your good.

Ps. 122.6–9

'Peace be upon Israel!' is a refrain of some of these later psalms. There is no more astonishing passage than the messianic vision of Isaiah.

> For a boy has been born for us, a son given to us
> > to bear the symbol of dominion on his shoulder;
> > and he shall be called
> > in purpose wonderful, in battle God-like,
> > Father for all time, Prince of peace.
> Great shall the dominion be,
> > and boundless the peace. . . .

Isa. 9.6–7

'Prince of peace' is almost an oxymoron, a contradiction in terms. Plenty of idealized heroes were 'God-like' in battle; a prince of peace was something new. It would be otiose to pursue the theme further. A vision of peace has crept upon a people of war.

RESISTANCE TO GREECE AND ROME

The resistance of the Maccabees to Antiochus Epiphanes and the Greek attempt to establish Greek culture and override Jewish religious susceptibilities provides a standard testimony for those who seek for examples of military involvement on behalf of the Jewish religion. It is important while recognizing this to observe also other aspects of the resistance at the time of the Maccabees. Active resistance there undoubtedly was, but there was also passive resistance by flight. Many went into the wilderness with 'their sons, and their wives, and their cattle', not as an act of guerrilla warfare, but as an act of withdrawal; they lived 'after the manner of wild beasts in the mountains'. The result was a falling off in tax revenues, the active policy of the government in seeking to bring them back,

85

and eventually an amnesty. Secondly, those who turned to violence became violent. Judas Maccabaeus actually fell in a civil war against his own people. It is significant that Judas is never mentioned in the *Talmud*. It has been supposed by some that this was due to Roman disapproval of the guerrillas. But it may equally have to do with the rabbinic emphasis on *shalom*. The festival of the Hannukah celebrates the Maccabean deliverance. Today it is sometimes an occasion of nationalistic and militaristic fervour. But the passage for reading on the Sabbath of Hannukah is from Zechariah: 'Not by might and not by power but by my spirit, saith the Lord of Hosts.'

So in the first and second centuries C.E. the people of Judaea rose against Rome. Their rising was disastrous, as Jesus of Nazareth foresaw that it would be. All along there were other voices. There were collaborators as well as guerrillas; there were the apolitical; there were advocates of passive resistance. Johanan ben Zakkai is an important figure. He belongs to the period of the Fall of Jerusalem in the first century C.E. One story tells how, in despair at the spirit of contention between different partisan groups, he had himself carried out of the city in a coffin to the Roman camp. Certainly he became persuaded that violent resistance merely contained within it the seeds of destruction. He was given permission by the Romans to establish a new centre at Jabneh-Jamnia for the study of the Torah, together with a court of justice. The school of Jabneh came to hold an authority comparable with that of the Sanhedrin earlier. Johanan's genius was to turn the leaders of Judaism from politics and acts of war to scholarship, piety and the things of peace, and to show that in so doing they were fulfilling rather than abandoning the central tenets of the faith.

THE TALMUD

'Seek peace and pursue it' became a central tenet of later Judaism. The *Talmud* points out how many of the commandments of the Law begin 'if' or 'when'. If the situation arises the believer's duty is clear, but he need not go out of his way to find the situation. 'In the case of peace, however, "Seek peace" wherever you happen to be, "and pursue it" if it is elsewhere.' The rabbinic exposition saw peace as part of God's original purpose for mankind. That was why he created initially a single individual. All mankind is thus essentially one (*Sanhedrin* 38a). So they stress peace. Thus Bar Kapparah: 'If the heavenly beings who are free from envy and hatred and rivalry are in need of peace, how much more are the lower beings, who are subject to hatred, rivalry and envy, in need of peace' (*Deut. Rabbah* 5, 12). Consider the following:

Beloved is peace, for God has given it both to those that answer and to those that are far off.

Deut. Rabbah 5, 15; Isa. 57.19

Great is peace, because peace is to the earth what yeast is to the dough.
If the Holy One, blessed be He, had not given peace to the earth, the sword and wild beasts would desolate the world.

Baraita de Perek ha-Shalom

Great is peace – for at the hour the Messiah reveals Himself to Israel, he will begin in no other way than with 'Peace'.

Ibid; Isa. 52.7

Great is peace, for it is equal to everything.

Numbers Rabbah 11, 7; Isa. 45.7

Great is peace, for God's name is peace.

Levit. Rabbah 9, 9; Judg. 6.24

Great is peace, because if the Jews were to practise idolatry, and peace prevailed among them at the same time, God would say, 'I cannot punish them, because peace prevails among them.'

Gen. Rabbah 38, 6

This is an astonishing affirmation. Peace takes precedence over one of the most solemn and basic of all the commandments. It is effectively a condemnation of Jehu, who massacred the Baal-worshippers, and of the Maccabees, who rose in violence against Greek idolatry. In general, peace is said to bring together in one all the blessings which God would heap on Israel.

So too the rabbis liked to put a peaceable interpretation upon stories of violence. Abraham's trained soldiers become scholars (Gen. 14.14; *Nedarim* 32a); so do Nebuchadnezzar's prisoners of war (2 Kings 24.16; *Sanhedrin* 38a). Jacob's sword and bow are treated as metaphorical for prayer and supplication (Gen. 48.22). David is remembered as a poet, musician and scholar rather than as a soldier and ruler.

One of the most remarkable of all such transformations comes in the Song of Deborah. Deborah is glorying in Jael's assassination of the tyrannical Sisera, and ends:

So perish all thine enemies, O Lord;
but let all who love thee be like the sun rising in strength.

Judg. 5.31

The rabbinic comment is:

They who are reviled but revile not others, they who hear themselves reproached but make no reply, they whose every act is one of love and who cheerfully bear their afflictions – these are the ones of whom Scripture says 'Those who love him are like the sun rising in strength'.

Yoma 23a; *Shabbat* 88b; *Gittin* 36b

The recurrence of this interpretation shows how highly it was valued; but it would be hard to imagine a more complete turnaround.

One particularly interesting comment relates to the ban on the use of hewn stone for altars (Exod. 20.25). There is almost a pun in the double meaning of *cherev*, sword or tool, but the rabbinic comment is unambiguous: 'Iron shortens life, whilst the altar prolongs it. The sword, or weapon of iron, is the symbol of strife; whereas the altar is the symbol of reconciliation and peace between God and man, and between man and his fellow' (*Mechilta Jethro* 5; *Sifra Kedoshin* 11, 8). Equally interesting is the treatment of the Feast of the Dedication (1 Macc. 4.59; 2 Macc. 10.6). This was an eight-day festival celebrating the rededication of the altar at Jerusalem after the Maccabean victories. The rabbis say nothing about the military triumph, stressing it as a Feast of Lights, and record a legend that they turned eight iron spears into candlesticks, a form of beating swords into mattocks (*Pesikta Rabati* 2).

The rabbis also condemn destructive action and praise constructive transformation. Forgiveness is better than revenge. As the *Talmud* has it, 'He who avenges himself or bears a grudge acts as one who has one hand cut by a knife, and then sticks it into the other hand for revenge.' There is awareness there alike of the solidarity of mankind and the tendency of violence to escalate. But if violence escalates so does goodness, kindness, friendliness. Philo, the Alexandrian Jew of the early Roman Empire, emphasizes this (*Virt.* 116–8). One rabbi illustrates it with a story of two rival donkey-drivers. One donkey falls under its load. The other driver takes the chance to get ahead, but then remembers the injunctions of the Torah and turns back to help, transforming rivalry into friendship (*Tanhuma Mishpatim* 1). There is a story of Rabbi Meir praying for the death of some highwaymen who were terrorizing the neighbourhood. His wife, Beruriah, herself a great expounder of Scripture, protested that such a prayer was illegitimate. 'It is written "Let sins cease". Is it written "Let sinners cease"? No, the word is "sins". At the end of the verse [Ps. 104.35] it goes on "and let the wicked men be no more". Once the sins have ceased, there will be no more wicked men! Rather pray that they will repent, and there will be no more wicked.' According to the story he changed his prayer – and they did repent. Similarly there is an excellent story of a Spanish Jew, Samuel ibn Nagrela. An enemy abused him in the king's presence. The king gave orders that Samuel should tear out the offender's foul tongue. Instead Samuel treated him with kindness and won his friendship. He justified himself to the king: 'I have torn out his angry tongue and given him a gentle one instead.' 'Who is the mightiest of heroes? He who makes his enemy his friend' (*Avot De- Rabbi Natan* 23). And this is true between nations as between individuals, between Israel and Egypt, for instance (*Deut. Rabbah* 5, 14).

Another general principle is that destructive action must be avoided if a less destructive action will suffice for the good end desired.

If one is able to save a victim at the cost of only a limb of the pursuer and does not take the trouble to do so, but saves the victim at the cost of the pursuer's life by killing him, he is deemed a shedder of blood and he deserves to be put to death. He may not, however, be put to death by the court because his true intention was to save life; he must be punished rather than put to death.

Mishneh Torah: Hilchot Rozeach 1, 13

That legislation is doubly notable in its humanity.

If destruction is ever necessary it is a tragic necessity, an occasion for sorrow, not for triumph. Life is sacred. 'Whoever sheds blood diminishes God's presence in the world' (*Gen. Rabbah* 34, 14). There are two excellent examples of this. One has to do with the deliverance from Egypt. The Egyptians are close in pursuit of the Israelites when the waters of the Red Sea come up and they are drowned. As the angels watch they want to raise a song of thanksgiving. But God will not have it. 'What? The work of my hands is drowning in the sea and you would chant hymns before me!' (*Sanhedrin* 39b). He does not save them from drowning; indeed he causes their drowning, but it is reluctantly and mirthlessly. From the same source comes an exposition due to Rabbi Jonathan. In Hebrew hymnody there is a famous refrain: 'Give thanks for the Lord, for it is good, for his mercy endures for ever' (e.g. Ps. 107.1). The phrase occurs in the account of a battle-muster before King Jehoshaphat (2 Chron. 20.21), but without the words, 'for it is good'. Why are they omitted? Because the destruction of human beings is not good. 'Because the Holy One, blessed be he, does not rejoice in the downfall of the wicked.'

War and the destruction of enemy soldiers are thus regarded by the rabbinical interpreters as in some circumstances an unfortunate necessity. They distinguished between two kinds of war, *milchemet reshut,* optional war, and *milchemet chovah*, obligatory war, also called *milchemet mitzvah*, religious war. This last included the war against the seven tribes of Canaan (Deut. 20.16–18), war against Amalek, who had been guilty of unprovoked aggression (Deut. 25.17–19), and defensive war generally. The seven tribes no longer exist; as Maimonides puts it, 'their memory has long perished', though some were found to argue that this justified military measures in establishing the modern state of Israel. The Amalekites have also disappeared, but all tyrants, dictators and oppressors have been considered to be 'the seed of Amalek'. 'The Lord will have war with Amalek from generation to generation' (Exod. 17.16), and many Jews justified military action against Hitler on these grounds. But the main grounds for a just war rest in attack from outside, and such a war is obligatory. There was much discussion among the rabbis as to whether preventive war fell in this category. The majority view was that it did not. 'Opinion is divided only when they engage their enemies in war because they are afraid that they will attack them, or if it is known that they are preparing to attack. According to Rabbi Judah it is obligatory and according to the sages it is optional' (*Sotah* 44b). Optional wars are much less clear morally, and the rabbis, though justifying those recorded in Scripture, have been far less ready to extend that justification to later wars. Their standard examples are the conquest of Canaan as an obligatory war, the expansions of the kingdom by David and his house as an optional war (ibid.). Maimonides sums up the whole doctrine concisely:

> The primary war which the King wages is a *religious war*. Which may be denominated a religious war? It includes the war against the seven tribes, the war against Amalek, and a war to deliver Israel from enemy aggression. Thereafter he may engage in an *optional war*, that is, a war against neighbouring nations to extend the borders of Israel and to enhance his greatness and prestige.

> *Mishneh Torah: Hilchot Melachim* 5, 1

But where the king can take full responsibility for declaring a religious war, an optional war requires the consent of the Sanhedrin.

Rabbinic tradition picked out the elements in the Torah which pointed to mercy and stressed these in their laws of war. Maimonides offers a convenient compendium. For example there was to be no wanton destruction.

> It is forbidden to cut down fruit-bearing trees outside a city, nor may a water channel be deflected from them so that they wither, as it is said: 'Thou shalt not destroy the trees thereof' (Deut. 20.19). Whoever cuts down a fruit-bearing tree is flogged. This penalty is imposed not only for cutting it down during a siege; whenever a fruit-yielding tree is cut down with destructive intent, flogging is

incurred. It may be cut down, however, if it causes damage to other trees or to a field belonging to another man or if its value for other purposes is greater. The law forbids only wanton destruction (ibid. 6, 8).

Not only one who cuts down trees, but also one who smashes household goods, tears clothes, demolishes a building, stops up a spring, or destroys articles of food with destructive intent, transgresses the command 'Thou shalt not destroy.' He is not flogged, but is administered a disciplinary beating imposed by the rabbis (ibid. 6, 10).

So too a woman prisoner is to be treated as a human being. She is to be allowed a period of mourning, during which she will appear less desirable. Then her captor may cohabit with her. But if she is converted to Judaism, then she will be ceremonially purified, and entitled to a legal marriage. And if he tires of her he must let her go freely, and is not entitled to enslave her or to sell her (ibid. 8, 5–6).

Sometimes the Rabbis go beyond the Torah. There is an instructive passage in Maimonides.

When siege is laid to a city for the purpose of capture, it may not be surrounded on all four sides but only on three in order to give an opportunity for escape to those who would flee to save their lives, as it is said: 'And they warred against Midian, as the Lord commanded Moses' (Num. 31.7). It has been learned by tradition that that was the instruction given to Moses (ibid. 6, 7).

We do not know where the tradition came from, but it is clearly not in the book of Numbers. Again, whereas the Bible decrees destruction without remission against Amalek and the seven tribes, the Rabbis dare to contradict the clear word of the Torah.

No war is declared against any nation before peace offers are made to it. This obtains both in an optional war and a religious war (ibid. 6, 1).

The other side are given the option of accepting the 'seven commandments enjoined upon the descendants of Noah'. These were: to avoid idolatry; to avoid blasphemy against the name of God;

to establish courts of justice; to avoid murder; to avoid adultery; to avoid theft; not to eat flesh cut from a living animal. As in Jewish tradition the whole human race was descended from Noah, these commandments were regarded as a kind of code of universal morality, and anyone who would not accept them was subhuman. But any people suing for peace, willing to pay tribute and to accept a subject status, and accepting these commandments must be left in peace.

> Once they make peace and take upon themselves the seven commandments, it is forbidden to deceive them and prove false to the covenant made with them (ibid. 6, 3).

Military service was in principle universal and compulsory, and in a religious war this applied even to a newly wedded bride. But in optional wars some exemptions from military service were permitted. These were on compassionate grounds. The three principal grounds for excusal were biblically based (Deut. 20.5–8). They were for those who had built (or, said the rabbis, come into possession of) a house but not yet occupied it; who had planted a vineyard but not yet enjoyed the fruit from it; or who were engaged to be married. Judas Maccabaeus in his concern for the Torah re-established the same principles (1 Macc. 3.56) despite the desperate military needs. Maimonides's compendium also reasserts them, but in such a way that they cannot be used as a trumped-up excuse. A small shack or a vineyard of four trees is not enough; illegal occupation does not count. Even more interesting, if a vineyard is jointly owned by two partners, neither is eligible for discharge. At the same time the rabbis added a further compassionate ground, that the death of one member of a family on military service exempts all his brothers. Those who receive exemption from military service are sometimes, though not always, liable to certain noncombatant duties in food-provision and road-repair (ibid. 7, 5–11). More radical than all these, however, is the Deuteronomic precept that the 'fearful and fainthearted' should be allowed to return home (Deut. 20.8). The reason given is that fear is infectious. There have been some attempts to interpret the words. *Rach halevav* could indicate a tender conscience, or a sensitivity to suffering in others, rather than cowardice. Rabbi Jose the Galilean took the whole phrase to mean those who were fearful because of their own misdeeds: it was better not to have guilty offenders in the army. But the more usual view is that of Rabbi Akiba: '"Fearful and fainthearted" is to be understood literally – he cannot endure the armies joined in battle or bear to see a drawn sword' (*Sotah* 8, 5).

> Our rabbis taught: If he heard the sound of trumpets and was panic-stricken, or beheld the brandishing of swords and the urine discharged itself upon his knees, he returns home (ibid. 44ab).

It is a more humane concession to human weakness than military discipline has generally allowed. And this is extended even to obligatory wars, where the other exemptions are disallowed. Further, some commentators claim that the priest anointed for war (the 'chaplain') is there precisely to assert the rights of this group.

Sabbath observance was another circumscription of military activity. It was one of the chief reasons why Jews were exempted from military service by the Romans (Jos. *Ant.* 14, 10, 11–19). The strict Jews would not bear arms on the Sabbath, and in the reign of Antiochus Epiphanes allowed themselves to be massacred rather than profane the Sabbath even in self-defence (1 Macc. 2.29–38). Once these scruples were known, military commanders opposed to the Jews took advantage of them (2 Macc. 5.25–6; 15.1; Jos. *Ap.* 1, 22; *Ant.* 13, 12, 4; 18, 9, 2). The Maccabaean guerrillas decided that there was no military future in strict observance at this point, and that they would fight defensively on the Sabbath, though they would not initiate battle (1 Macc. 2.41; 9.34–49; 2 Macc. 8.21–8; cf. Jos. *BJ* 2, 18, 2). This last remained a severe restriction: for example the Jewish troops would not destroy siegeworks on the Sabbath, and it was this which enabled Pompey to complete his preparations against Jerusalem (Jos. *Ant.* 14, 4, 2). Rabbinic tradition did not go much further than prohibiting the declaration of an optional war on the Sabbath.

In general, while war was permitted, the rabbis did not allow their disciples to forget that war was justified only if directed to constructive ends, which would be lost if standards of behaviour were allowed to slide. Maimonides puts it excellently in his *Guide to the Perplexed* (3, 41).

It will thus be confirmed in the heart of every one of the Israelites that their camp must be like a sanctuary of the Lord, and it must not be like the camps of the heathen, whose sole object is corruption and sin, and who seek only to cause injury to others and to take their property, whilst our object is to lead mankind to the service of God and to a good sound order.

One further point in the Jewish traditions is that there is a general obligation for the individual to be actively involved on the side of good against evil. He is invited to regard the world as nicely balanced between the two. His action may turn the scale.

He who commits a good deed may incline the balance with regard to himself and all mankind towards the side of the good: and he who commits a sin may incline the balance with regard to himself and all mankind towards the side of guilt.

Tosefta Kiddushin 1, 13

So:

Whoever is able to protest against the transgressions of his own family and does not do so is punished for the transgressions of his family. Whoever is able to protest against the transgressions of the people of his community and does not do so is punished for the transgressions of his community. Whoever is able to protest against the transgressions of the entire world and does not do so is punished for the transgressions of the entire world.

Sanhedrin 54b

And again:

If the man of learning participates in public affairs and serves as judge or arbitrator, he gives stability to the land. But if he sits in his home and says to himself, 'What have the affairs of society to do with me? . . . Why should I trouble myself with the people's voices of protest? Let my soul dwell in peace!' – if he does this, he overthrows the world.

Tanhuma Mishpatim

If the community is in trouble, a man must not say, 'I will go to my house, and eat and drink, and peace shall be with thee, O my soul.' But a man must share in the trouble of the community even as Moses did. He who shares in its troubles is worthy to see its consolation.

Taanit 11a

There is in fact a duty to act to help others in need.

Whence do we know that if you see your fellow drowning in the river or attacked by robbers or by a vicious animal that it is your duty to save his life? It says, 'You shall not stand idly by the blood of your neighbour.'

Sanhedrin 73a; Lev. 19.16

This may lead to the taking of life.

A man who pursues another to kill him, or after a male, or after a betrothed girl, may be delivered at the cost of their lives.

Sanhedrin 8, 7

The deliverance is of course from sin. Judaism thus does not countenance quietism, and fosters active involvement.

A VOCATION TO SUFFERING

Across the centuries the Jewish people have suffered intensely from persecution. From this has come the idea of a vocation to suffering, of the acceptance of suffering, not the infliction of suffering, as a means of changing the world. One great rabbinic dictum was 'Be of the persecuted rather than of the persecutors' (*Baba Kamma* 93a). So Rabbi Joshua ben Levi said, 'He who gladly accepts the sufferings of this world brings salvation to the world.' So Judah Ha Levi in *al Khuzari* (11, 44) in the twelfth century wrote that Israel has a mission of suffering. Israel, the heart of humanity, the suffering servant, bears the ills of all, and by this very fact allows God to reveal Himself on earth. Simon ben Yochai said, 'The best which God gave Israel, he gave through suffering.' 'God be thanked', cried Sholem Asch, 'that the nations have not given my people the opportunity to commit against others the crimes which have been committed against it.' The vocation of suffering is the theme of André Schwarz-Barth's Prix Goncourt novel *The Last of the Just*:

> And praised. Auschwitz. So be it. Maidenek. The Eternal. Treblinka. And praised. Buchenwald. So be it. Mauthausen. The Eternal. Belzec. And praised. Sobibor. So be it. Chelnino. The Eternal. Ponary. And praised. Theresienstadt. So be it. Warsaw. The Eternal. Wilno. And praised. Skarzysko. So be it. Bergen-Belsen. The Eternal. Janow. And praised. Dora. So be it. Neuengamme. The Eternal. Pustkow. And praised . . .

TWO PRAYERS

Rabbi Hirsch ends his excellent little study with two prayers, slightly paraphrased. The first is the *Sam Shalom*, the traditional prayer for peace.

> Grant us peace, thy most precious gift, O thou eternal source of peace, and enable Israel to be its messenger to the peoples of the earth. Bless our country that it may ever be a stronghold of peace, and its advocate in the council of nations. May contentment reign within its borders, health and happiness within its homes. Strengthen the bonds of friendship and fellowship among the inhabitants of all lands. Plant virtue in every soul, and may the love of thy name hallow every home and every heart. Praised be thou, O Lord, Giver of peace.

The other, the *Alenu* prayer, is an act of adoration for the close of every service.

> May the time not be distant, O God, when thy name shall be worshipped in all the earth, when unbelief shall disappear and error be no more. Fervently we pray that the day may come when all men shall invoke thy name, when corruption and evil shall give way to purity and goodness, when superstition shall no longer enslave the mind, nor idolatry blind the eye, when all who dwell on earth shall know that to thee alone every knee must bend and every tongue give homage. O may all, created in thine image,

recognize that they are brethren, so that, one in spirit and one in fellowship, they may be forever united before thee. Then shall thy kingdom be established on earth and the word of thine ancient seer be fulfilled. The Lord will reign for ever and ever.

FOR FURTHER READING

Braden, Chas S., *War, Communism and the World's Religions*. Harper and Row, 1953.

Dakin, D. M., *Peace and Brotherhood in the Old Testament*. Bannisdale Press, 1956.

Ferguson, J., *The Place of Suffering*. C.U.P., 1972.

Hirsch, R. G., *Thy Most Precious Gift: Peace in Jewish Tradition*. New York, Union of American Hebrew Congregations, 1974.

Loewe, R., ed., *Studies in Rationalism, Judaism and Universalism*. Routledge, 1966.

Chapter 7

CHRISTIANITY

JESUS THE MESSIAH

Christianity was nurtured in the cradle of Judaism, and the Christian approach to war and peace is not to be understood apart from the political situation of the first century C.E. and the messianic expectations of the time.

Let us remember. Jerusalem was destroyed in 586 B.C. and the inhabitants deported. Fifty years later Babylon fell to Persia and they were allowed to return. They continued subject to Persia for two centuries, then after Alexander's coming were subject to Greek dynasties, the Seleucids of Antioch and the Ptolemies of Egypt. The extreme Hellenizing policy of Antiochus Epiphanes led to revolt, and the accidents of history produced nearly a century of quasi-independence under the Hasmoneans, which aroused a continuing desire for an independence which seemed always improbable but never impossible. The coming of Pompey in 63 B.C. was the effective end of independence, though it dragged on in an attenuated form for the next quarter of a century; these years saw continual violent uprisings, by Alexander in 57, Aristobulus and Antigonus in 56, Alexander again in 55, Pitholaus in 52, Antigonus in 41. In the end Herod the Idumaean, a hated foreigner, came out on top. His death in 4 B.C. was followed by a troubled three-quarters of a century, with Rome either in the background or in the forefront. There was open revolt associated with the census of 6 C.E. The tactless anti-Semitism of Pontius Pilate, procurator between 26 and 36 C.E., fired several disturbances. In 66 full war broke out and led eventually to the sack of Jerusalem.

Israel of old had been a theocracy, a single political and religious community. After the death of Solomon the Kingdom divided. The disasters of 721 B.C. and 586 B.C. further broke the unity. There came an apocalyptic dream in which the Messiah, the Anointed, was to be the deliverer, the liberator, God's vice-gerent in the restored kingdom. As T. W. Manson put it, 'The religious soul of Israel must find a body. Hence the Messianic hope, the hope of restoring on a higher level the unity of national life that had been broken at the Exile.'

There was a strong tradition that the Messiah would be a military leader. This appears in the Old Testament, where the Messiah will break the nations with a rod of iron (Ps. 2.9) and shatter the yoke which fetters Israel (Is. 9.4–5). It is especially strong in the literature of the period just before or contemporary with Jesus. For example, in 2 Esdras 12.31–3 the Messiah is the lion who is to destroy the Roman Empire. The most extreme account of the military Messiah is in Ezra 4, where the Messiah is the merciless conqueror of the Gentiles. But the general tenor of the apocalyptic of the period is that though the messianic kingdom would be a peaceable kingdom it would be imposed by force. This is clear not least in the number of messianic pretenders who raised the flag of violent revolt (Acts 5. 35–9).

The expectation that Jesus might be the Messiah runs through the gospel story, most strongly in John. John the Baptist refused the title for himself; another is the true Messiah. Andrew goes to Peter with the words 'We have found the Messiah'. A woman from Samaria asks 'Can this be the Messiah?' The people try to proclaim him king; they are talking about him as the Messiah. In the other Gospels his leading follower, Simon Peter, openly calls him the Messiah and is praised for his inspiration. Jesus's entry into Jerusalem is a messianic entry. He was executed as King of the Jews, taunted with being Messiah. No doubt some of his followers came to him in that expectation – Simon the Zealot (a word which meant 'freedom-fighter' by the time the Gospels were written), perhaps Judas Iscariot (the Latin *sicarius* means 'dagger-man'), Simon Peter Bar-Jona (which may mean 'son of John' but which was also a revolutionary nickname).

59078

But Jesus did not behave like a military Messiah. In the wilderness he was tempted by Satan to possess the kingdoms of the world on terms not God's; in context this must mean the temptation to political power by military means, and Jesus rejected it. The kingdom which he proclaimed was not a new political state but the sovereignty of God. He rejected the violent policies of the liberation movement. If he drew some of them to him, he equally drew a collaborator, a hated tax-collector. No Zealot would have healed a Roman soldier or commended a Roman soldier's faith, or told his followers, in a context which referred explicitly to the Romans, to 'love your enemies'. Jesus took five thousand men into the countryside; it looked like the beginning of a military-political operation, but he gave them a lesson in practical community and sent them away again. When Peter proclaimed him the Messiah he taught that he would suffer and, when Peter protested, called him Satan, renewing the temptation in the wilderness. Jesus seems to have been the first person to identify the Messiah with the Servant who Suffers, depicted in Isaiah. For his messianic entry he took up one of the few prophetic passages which show a non-military Messiah (Zechariah 9.9–10), and rode into Jerusalem on a donkey, to bring not war but peace. His prophecies of the fall of Jerusalem and destruction of the Temple were deeply shocking. He could see the simple human truth that violence escalates, and that the violent uprising on which his people were set would lead to a still more violent suppression. At the same time he proclaimed a messianic hope which was not centred on Jerusalem and the Temple. In Gethsemane he was arrested. Some think that Judas was trying to force his hand into armed revolt (for the betrayal bribe was nugatory). In any event he refused armed support and declared, 'All those who take the sword shall perish by the sword', disowning even defensive warfare and (as Tertullian was to put it) disarming every soldier. He allowed himself to be executed, and Christians claim that he rose from the dead, and through the 'baptism' of death, his Spirit was no longer confined to one human body, but could operate through the whole body of the Church; he conquered through suffering.

The way of life proclaimed and demonstrated by Jesus is summed up in the word 'love', *agape*. Christians claim that 'God is love' (1

John 4.8), that Jesus is the perfect revelation of the God who is love, the eternal Logos or Word, the expression of the Mind of God (John 1.1–14), the Son of God (John 1.34 etc.), that is the one who is wholly identified with God, as Son of Lies means an utter and complete liar; also that the way of the Cross, itself laid upon his followers (Mark 8.34), is the exemplification of the way of love to which they are called. The way of love is expounded by the ablest mind among the early Christians, Paul, in writing his letters to Roman and Corinthian Christians, and in the record of Jesus's teaching preserved in the so-called Sermon on the Mount. A few quotations will illustrate this:

> Repay no one evil for evil, but take thought for what is noble in the sight of all. If possible, so far as it depends upon you, live peaceably with all. Beloved, never avenge yourselves, but leave it to God; for it is written, 'Vengeance is mine, I will repay, says the Lord.' No, 'If your enemy is hungry, feed him; if he is thirsty, give him drink; for by so doing you will heap burning coals upon his head.' Do not be overcome by evil, but overcome evil with good.
>
> Paul in Rom. 12.17–21

> Love is patient and kind; love is not jealous or boastful; it is not arrogant or rude. Love does not insist on its own way; it is not irritable or resentful; it does not rejoice at wrong, but rejoices in the right. Love bears all things, believes all things, hopes all things, endures all things.
>
> Paul in 1 Cor. 13.4–7

> You have heard that it was said 'You shall love your neighbour and hate your enemy'. But I say to you 'Love your enemies, and pray for those who persecute you' so that you may be sons of your Father who is in heaven; for he makes his sun rise upon the evil and the good, and sends rain on the just and on the unjust. For if you love those who love you what reward have you? Do not even the tax-collectors do the same? And if you salute only your brethren, what more are you doing than others? Do not even the Gentiles do the same? You, therefore, must be perfect (comprehensive in your love), as your heavenly Father is perfect.
>
> Jesus in Matt. 5.43–8

Blessed are the peacemakers, for they shall be called the sons of God.

Jesus in Matt. 5.9

It is clear in these passages that to the Christian love is the very being of God, and therefore the depth of the being and only true fulfilment of those who are made in the image of God; that it is not an ideal aspiration but a practical path in a world of violence and evil; that it is concerned with means as well as ends, and involves a refusal to meet violence and evil with violence and evil; that its ultimate 'weapon' is suffering; and that it has to do with political and group relationships and not merely with personal encounters. This last is important. Jesus in telling his followers 'Love your enemy' says, 'You have heard it said in the past, you shall love your neighbour and hate your enemy.' It was not of the Jewish dispensation to hate a personal enemy, and the whole context speaks of the Romans.

THE EARLY CHURCH

The New Testament is a document of the early Christian Church, and a record not merely of the life and teaching of Jesus but of the beliefs and practices of Christians fifty years later. The simple fact is that for something like a century and a half after the ministry of Jesus, Christians would not touch military service, and for more than another century the predominant sense continued that Christianity and war were incompatible. Christians were charged with undermining the Roman Empire by refusing military service and public office; they answered that human life was sacred to them, that they were the race given over to peace, that God prohibits killing even in a just cause, without exception, that the weapons of the Christian were prayer, justice and suffering. Even in the fifth century C.E., after the weight of a nominally Christian state authority had been placed in the balance against pacifism for nearly a century, one of Augustine's correspondents is still complaining that Christian refusal of military service is endangering the empire.

Two factors exercised a pull in the opposite direction. First, from about 173 C.E. we can trace a certain number of Christians in the army. They were always a small proportion until well into the fourth century; only at the end of that century can Theodosius purge the army of pagans. We can be fairly certain that Christians in the army were soldiers converted to Christianity during their period of service. Church orders from a later period, but incorporating earlier traditions, show that no catechumen or believer might join the army, that soldier-converts were required to refuse to kill, even if commanded to do so (we must remember that this was the period of 'the immeasurable majesty of the Roman peace', and many soldiers would never see battle, but were engaged in constructive building operations), and that serving soldiers could not become full Church members until after they had left the army. In the fourth century Martin of Tours, converted while a soldier, stayed in his normal duties till battle was joined, then said 'I am a soldier of Christ; I cannot fight', offering to show his sincerity by going out into the front line armed only with a cross.

Second, Cicero, a Roman pagan of the first century B.C., had explored the concept of the just war. This involved three factors. There must be just cause, there must be formal declaration of war by the constituted authority, and the war must be conducted justly. Some kind of doctrine of the just war is taken up by the Christian apologists, Tertullian and Origen. But it is not accepted as having any validity for Christians. Tertullian and Origen were alike firm that the Christian might not be associated with the taking of life 'even justly'. But both of them allow a relative justification of violent acts for good motives in pre-Christian days or among non-Christians, rather as Gandhi was later to do. What they were saying to their pagan critics was 'The standard laid upon us as Christians is to take no part in war; this we fulfil. The standard laid upon you as pagans is to take no part in any save just wars; you had best be careful that you fulfil this.' But they opened the door for Ambrose and Augustine to apply this standard to the nominally Christian empire of their own day.

CONSTANTINE

The turning-point was the conversion of Constantine. His family were worshippers of the Unconquered Sun. He was himself born to the purple, and called to it by the will of his father's soldiers. When he was marching to secure the supreme power for himself he saw a cross in the sky superimposed on the sun, a rare but attested version of the halo-phenomenon, and the words came to him, 'triumph in this'. He put on his soldiers' shields the chi-rho, a pattern of cross and circle spelling the first two letters of the name of Christ in Greek, and he did indeed triumph. It was a call to syncretism, a Christian symbol coming from the sun. His family had been tolerant of Christianity, and Constantine now brought in official policies of tolerance. The Christians began to taste worldly power and wealth. Meantime Constantine did not reject his past. Pagan gods were still officially honoured, pagan symbols appeared on his coins. Even when he established the new capital of Constantinople, the Fortune of the City was still honoured and Constantine's own statue set up with the rayed crown of the Sun-god formed, as he believed, from the nails with which Christ was crucified. Syncretism could go no further. Constantine was baptized only on his death-bed. He was not wholly insincere, though he was ruthless in the pursuit of power. But his understanding of Christianity was limited and his god was always a god of power, never a god of love.

The fortunes of the Church were now tied up with the fortunes of the state. The fact that Christ's coming lay in the reign of Augustus led to a theory of the providence of God equally at work in both. Yet the pacifism of Christ's teaching remained. So in Eusebius, writing under Constantine, we see a new theory emerging which, in fact, separates full Christian obedience from the political realm. According to this view there are two levels of Christian vocation. The clergy are to be totally dedicated to God and to live in accordance with the fullness of life shown in the New Covenant; the laity are to exercise the normal obligations of citizenship.

The implications of this are first worked out by Ambrose and Augustine. Ambrose, bishop of Milan, a former Roman administrator, prayed for the victory of the Roman armies, identifying the invading Goths with the evil figure of Gog. The Old Testament is never far from his thought. The Church and empire were interdependent; the defence of the empire was a kind of holy war. But Ambrose, though less scrupulous than his more refined theories in dealing with heretical barbarians, applied Cicero's just war doctrines, buttressed by the Old Testament, to form a Christian philosophy of war. This was in turn taken up by Augustine, bishop of Hippo Regius in Africa. Augustine claimed on the basis of the Old Testament that war was the instrument of divine judgement on wickedness, and tried to reconcile this with the obviously divergent teachings of the New Testament by interpreting the latter in an inward and spiritual sense, and by insisting on absolute pacifism in personal relations. He remained somewhat puzzled by the Sermon on the Mount, and laid much stress upon the natural order. Augustine further enlarged Cicero's doctrine of the just war by turning it into a kind of penal sanction. So righteousness became justice, and justice was interpreted in terms of law; love was left as an inner disposition which might be a proper motive for punishing a sinner. Augustine's teaching about war arises ultimately from his doctrine of sin and punishment. Augustine, though well aware of the horrors of war, and sceptical about power politics, actually dissuaded General Boniface from his immediate intention to become a monk; there was soldier's work to do first. At the same time he told him that the object of war was peace.

THE DARK AGES

During the centuries which followed it is not easy to discern that the New Testament made much difference to the public behaviour of lay Christians. A famous story of Clovis, military hero of the Franks, tells how he learned of the crucifixion and said, 'If I and my Franks had been there, it would never have happened.' The Franks – or their first-century equivalents – were not there precisely because Jesus chose that they should not be there. But Clovis and his Franks went their ruthless way after his conversion to Catholic Christianity. The oldest surviving German poem actually exalts Simon Peter for drawing the sword in Gethsemane. Charlemagne fought against pagans and infidels with the papal blessing; military force compelled the conversion of the Saxons; even the clergy fought in these wars. As a rule, however, the clergy did not participate. The Synod of Ratisbon in 742 pronounced, 'We absolutely and in all circumstances forbid all God's servants to carry arms, to fight, and to march against an army or against an enemy.' A century later Agobard of Lyons invited the soldiers of Christ to demonstrate their faith not by killing but by dying. The Council of Meaux in 845 declared: 'Those who are members of the clergy are not to take up or to carry arms . . . for they cannot be at the same time soldiers of the world and soldiers of God.' Pope Nicholas I (858–67) wrote: 'The soldiers of the world are distinct from the soldiers of the Church. Hence it is unfitting to the soldiers of the Church to fight for the affairs of the world, which involves them inevitably in the shedding of blood.' Pope John VIII (872–82) wrote: 'It is absolutely opposed to the service of bishops and priests and to the dignity of their character to engage in warfare.' There was sometimes a curious literalism. In 1182 Christian, Archbishop of Mainz, fought in battle with a mace, killing nine men, to avoid the stain of bloodshed through the use of a sword.

Even with the laity there was a continuing sense that the shedding of blood was incompatible with the New Testament and required expiation, and penitentials, such as that of Egbert (c. 750) or Reginon of Prum (c. 915), prescribe a forty-day penance for those who kill a man even in open battle under superior orders. The Arundel Penitential actually prescribes a one-year penance for the taking of life in a just war. But attitudes were very ambivalent. Hincmar of Rheims held that those who died faithfully in war merited prayers, offerings, and masses. Pope Leo IV, in the turbulent ninth century, supported the Frankish armies and expressed the hope that those who died in defence of the faith would merit eternal life. Later in the same century John VIII promised indulgences to those who died fighting infidels and pagans.

Western Europe during the so-called Dark Ages was in fact racked with wars both internal and external, from major international wars to petty private feuds. In the tenth century the Archbishop of Bordeaux attempted to control the devastation by initiating the Peace of God, to exempt from violence certain specified noncombatants, such as the clergy, women, unarmed peasants and merchants. In the following century the Truce of God was an attempt to put an end to the unbroken hostilities by limiting them in time. The principles varied slightly, but in general there was to be no fighting from Thursday to Sunday each week in honour of Christ's sufferings, none at all in the Advent and Christmas seasons and during Lent and the period from Easter to Pentecost. Robert the Pious (996–1031) took an oath to observe both the Peace and the Truce. It is not clear how effective this movement was.

CRUSADES

Another solution lay in the Crusades. These were an attempt to discourage internecine strife by concentrating military energy on a single external enemy under the guidance and blessing of the papacy. This can be clearly seen in the policies of Gregory VII (1073–85). In 1093 Urban II promulgated the Truce of God, and at Clermont two years later pronounced it a law of the Church, at the same time initiating the First Crusade, the righteous war against the infidel, promising those who participated blessings in heaven and the temporal rewards of booty. This was not Augustine's just war; it was more akin to Augustine's use of the secular arm to suppress heresy. But it was a course of action which enabled a man as spiritually sensitive and profound as Bernard of Clairvaux to divert the pacifistic message to the cause of war and to make bellicosity seem almost a mystical virtue. Monastic pacifism was soft-pedalled, and the monastic military orders of the Templars, Hospitallers and Knights of St John emerged.

The Crusades had behind them a strong element of high idealism. Probably no religion, not even Islam, has ever launched quite such an intensive succession of holy wars. But their motives were complex; they have been seen, for example, as a continuation in the movement of the Teutonic peoples of central Europe, and as an anticipation of the later expansiveness of western Europe. One of the Crusades actually became an attack on Christian Constantinople and had the effect of weakening the defences of Christendom against Islam. The Crusaders in general left Muslims with the picture of Christians as militaristic imperialists, and the life in the Crusaders' camps did much to increase their contempt for Christian moral indiscipline. Roger Bacon was among those who held the Crusades to be both cruel and useless; the infidel should be converted, not attacked, and would be more open to conversion if the Christians were less aggressive and rapacious.

GRATIAN AND THE JUST WAR

About 1140 a monk named Gratian compiled a volume entitled *Concordia Discordantium Canonum* but generally known as *Decretum*. This is a major document in the history of Christian thinking about the Just War. Gratian takes off from Augustine and Roman law. According to him military service is not inherently sinful; its proper purposes are to repel injuries and to inflict punishment. A war is just if undertaken to repel enemy aggression or to recover stolen property; to avenge injuries through an authoritative edict; to assert a legal right. It requires authority, obedience, and a just cause. But Gratian is imprecise in defining legal authority, and still more imprecise in his remarks upon just means, though he declares immunity for clergy, women, pilgrims, monks and the unarmed poor.

Gratian introduced the concept of the Just War into modern international jurisprudence. His views were taken up by Rufinus in 1157. Rufinus tried to sharpen Gratian's definition. A war was just in terms of three people: the declarer, the soldier and the enemy. It must be declared by properly constituted authority, fought with worthy zeal, directed against a guilty party. Other followers of Gratian sharpened other parts of his definition. Huguccio, for example, being strongly of the opinion that wars of aggression were unjust, wars of defence just. But Huguccio also developed out of the Old Testament interpreted in terms of Roman law a doctrine of a religiously motivated just war against heretics and infidels who by their opposition to divine law were denied the protection of human law. It was an all-too-convenient doctrine in the age of Crusades. In the mid-thirteenth century Hostiensis distinguished seven types of war: (i) the 'Roman' war, a just war waged by the faithful against infidels; (ii) a judicial war, waged by Christians on just authority; (iii) unjust war waged in defiance of legitimate authority; (iv) just war waged by proper authority to repel injury from others; (v) unjust war waged against legal authority; (vi) unjust war waged for private ends; (vii) just war to repel the last.

It would be idle to go through all the arguments and refinements produced in the Middle Ages, though it is interesting to note that the Second Lateran Council in 1139 forbade the use of crossbows, bows and arrows and siege machines in wars against other Christians: these were the atomic bombs of the twelfth century, indiscriminate in their destruction, and irresistible in their power, 'deadly and odious to God'. One suspects that the fact that they were manned by the commons but might destroy the nobility had something to do with it. This is important as an attempt to control the means of war; some people held that in a just war all was fair.

The Franciscans show the ambiguities of the period clearly. They were among the foremost exponents of the view that the Crusades were not the right way to spread the Christian gospel among Muslims; they were among the most dynamic missionaries of the age. The whole tenor of Francis's approach to life was pacifist. Yet it was Franciscan theologians who were particularly concerned with precise formulation of the Just War doctrine. They analysed the requirements into five or six: person, circumstances, cause, intention and authority according to one formulation; authority, attitude, intention, condition, merit and cause according to another. If any one of these was deficient the war was unjust.

The monumental genius of Thomas Aquinas brought the whole doctrine into a clearer and more systematic form, expressed in Aristotelian concepts which in his day were revolutionary. Aquinas began by countering the obvious pacifist interpretation of the New Testament. To the statement that all those who take the sword shall perish by the sword he asserted that this did not apply to those in public authority. To the words 'Resist not evil' he gave an inward and spiritual interpretation, and claimed the primacy of the common good. To the exaltation of peace he answered that just wars are undertaken for the sake of peace. A just war requires authority, and primarily the mandate of a prince charged with the common good; a just cause, primarily a guilty enemy; and a just intention, to promote good or to avoid evil. This last extended the application of the criteria from ends to means. Aquinas's achievement was to bring together Augustine's concept of war as a punishment for sin and the Aristotelian emphasis on the common good. It formed a bridge between the knightly warrior and the standing army.

The formulation of the Just War was finalized by three great Catholic theologians of the sixteenth century: Vitoria, Bellarmine and Suarez. There were four basic criteria: (i) it must be proclaimed by lawful authority; (ii) the cause must be just; (iii) the belligerents should have a rightful intention, to advance good or avoid evil; (iv) the war must be fought by proper means. Additional criteria are sometimes found; (v) action should be against the guilty; (vi) the innocent should not suffer (this was usually interpreted to mean that they should not suffer anything irreparable such as loss of life); (vii) war must be undertaken as a last resort; (viii) there must be a reasonable chance of success.

It is hard not to see in the doctrine of the Just War a conformity of the Church to the unredeemed standards of the world. It was an attempt, accepting the fact of war, to keep it under control. It was an immeasurable support to those in power, for any violence against them was automatically unjust; it was a consolidation of the authority of pope, emperor and kings, who were granted a monopoly of violence. But it was subject to two major disadvantages. First, there was no objective tribunal to declare a cause just. The authority declaring the 'just' war is advocate, judge, jury and executioner. If, as the Christian writer Roland Bainton has put it, all war is 'self-vindication without due process of law', then the doctrine of the Just War gives a veneer of self-justification but not an atom of legality. Second, it seems to have very little to do with the Christian faith. The arguments of Augustine or Aquinas are a replacement of the teaching of the New Testament by Greek philosophy or Roman law. There is nothing, literally nothing, distinctively Christian about the result. Yet these are the considerations which have dominated the majority of Christians for most of the history of the Church.

GROUPS OF THE REFORMATION

When we come to the period of the Renaissance and Reformation the story becomes inordinately complex. In the later Middle Ages there were a number of pacifist groups, mostly among the unorthodox sectaries. Such were to be found among the Waldensians, a group of whom were persuaded to return to the Church and were granted exemption from military service. Such were the Cathari, who refused to take animal life, believing in transmigration, though some of them defended themselves with violence when attacked. Such was Wycliffe's follower Nicholas of Hereford, who declared, 'Jesus Christ, duke of oure batel, taught us lawe of pacience and not to fight bodily.' In 1395 the Lollards presented to Parliament their Twelve Conclusions. The tenth condemns war:

'The tende conclusion is, that manslaute be batayle ... with outen special revelaciun is expres contrarious to the newe testament, the qwiche is a lawe of grace and ful of mercy. This conclusion is opinly procud be exsample of Cristis preching here in erthe, the qwiche most taute for to love and to have mercy on his enemys, and nout for to slen them ... The lawe of mercy, that is the new testament, forbad al mannislaute ... be mekenesse and suffraunce our beleve was multiplied, and fythteres and mansleeris Ihesu Crist hatith ...

So too the Hussites in Czecho-Slovakia, owing as they did a debt to Wycliffe, developed through the leadership of Peter Czelcicky (c. 1390–1460) a pacifist wing. These Brethren of the Law of Christ resolved that they would not defend themselves by the use of armed violence.

New peace groups emerged in the sixteenth and seventeenth centuries. They were very various. Some were humanist. Christian humanism was not incompatible with nationalistic militarism, as we can see in Zwingli or Ulrich von Hutten. But on the whole the weight of humanism is in the other scale. Erasmus was the foremost exponent of this humanistic pacifism. In theory, as a loyal Catholic he subscribed to the doctrine of the Just War; in practice he did not allow any of the wars of his time to be just. His celebrated tract *The Complaint of Peace* is a blend of classical humanism and New Testament Christianity, a passionate deprecation of the horrors of war and plea for commitment to the Christ who is Prince of Peace.

Erasmus did not stand alone. Agrippa of Nettesheim listed the horrors of war, whose 'whole art studies nothing else but the subversion of Mankind, transforming men into beasts and monsters so that War is nothing but a general Homicide and Robbery by mutual Consent'. He attacked 'the many Orders of Holy Soldiers, all whose religion consists in Blood, Slaughter, Rapine and Pyracy, under pretence of defending and enlarging the *Christian faith*'; 'Christ and his Apostles teach quite another doctrine.'

Of more ultimate importance in Christian history are the so-called historic peace churches, the Anabaptists (surviving as Mennonites and Hutterites), the Brethren, and the Religious Society of Friends (popularly known as Quakers). They are often grouped together, and with all of them the refusal of war is based on their understanding of the New Testament and of the way of Jesus. But their pacifism has taken very different forms. The Anabaptists have tended to remain aloof from political responsibility. They have been termed 'apolitical'; John C. Bennett, a noted non-pacifist, sees the Mennonites as the outstanding example of the 'strategy of withdrawal'. On the other hand the Quakers have tended towards political involvement. The name of William Penn is an obvious example. In the Quaker approach to peace and war there has been a strong element of redemptive personalism, based theologically on the concept of 'that of God in every man'. Penn wrote in 1684, 'Governments rather depend upon men than men upon governments. Let men be good, and government cannot be bad. If it be ill, they will cure it. But if men be bad, let the government be ever so good, they will endeavour to warp and spoil it to their tune.' So Quakers start from personal testimony; among their 'Queries' is 'Are you faithful in maintaining our testimony against all war as inconsistent with the spirit and teaching of Christ? Do you live in the life and power that takes away the occasion of all wars?' But Quakers were equally firm about the political consequences of their personal commitment. George Fox said, 'We love all men and women, simply as they are men and women and as they are God's workmanship, and so as brethren'; the consequence of this for William Penn was that he went unarmed to meet the American Indians and to sign a treaty with them.

113

Fox's refusal to fight for Cromwell was expressed in classic words: 'I live in the virtue of that life and power that takes away the occasion of all wars.' William Dewsbury had seen the war against the King as a Crusade, but then heard the word of the Lord say to him 'Put up thy sword into thy scabbard', and came to realize that he must use only spiritual weapons. So Isaac Pennington: 'Fighting is not suitable to a gospel spirit, but to the spirit of the world and the children thereof.' So Friends disowned what Fox called 'carnal weapons'. There were other factors, as General Monk ruefully observed. People who believe in conscientious decisions are not good at blind obedience, people who believe in social equality disrupt the distinction between officer and private soldier, and people who respect the conscience of others find it hard to see the issues of war in black and white. At the same time this very fact gave Friends a respect for the conscience of soldiers. When Penn, an aristocrat whose sword was an emblem of rank, became worried about carrying a lethal weapon and consulted Fox, Fox advised him, 'Wear it as long as thou canst.' This applied to serving soldiers. When their conscience was convicted, it would constrain them to give up the sword.

In many ways the profoundest of the reformation pacifists was the leader of the Swiss Brethren, Conrad Grebel. Grebel's attitude was rooted in his understanding of the New Testament. He stood by a commitment to absolute, non-resisting love, and rejected all forms of war and violence, personal and political. This understanding was not based upon the isolation of a few texts, but upon a total view, and particularly on the concept of the suffering Church. So Grebel and his associates wrote to the militant Thomas Münzer, 'The Gospel and those who accept it are not to be protected by the sword, nor are they thus to protect themselves. . . . Truly believing Christians are sheep among wolves, sheep for the slaughter; anguish and affliction, tribulation, persecution, suffering and death must be their baptism; they must be tried with fire, and must reach the fatherland of eternal rest, not by killing them bodily, but by mortifying their spiritual enemies. Neither do they use worldly sword or war, since by them killing is entirely abrogated.' Grebel added a personal postscript to Münzer, 'If you are willing to defend war, then I admonish you not to do so. . . . And if you must suffer for it, know well that it cannot be otherwise. Christ must yet more suffer in His members. But He will strengthen and keep them steadfast to the end.'

These were all small minority groups, though influential beyond their numbers. On the whole the Protestant Reformers began from the Just War doctrine. The Church of England may be taken as typical: 'It is lawfull for Christian men, at the commandment of the Magistrate, to weare weapons and serve in the warres.' Luther offered a sharp dichotomy between the state and the Church, both ordained by God, the minister of state being armed with the sword, the minister of the Church with the Word. Luther believed that both were instruments of Christian love, which operated differently in different spheres; he 'would not have the gospel defended by violence and murder', but regarded the pacifism of Jesus as no more binding on his followers than his celibacy or his carpentry. The Christian must not fight the Turk for religious reasons, but the Emperor might fight the Turk for political reasons. Further, the rejection of the monastic calling gave a stronger sense of divine vocation to lay occupations, including that of the soldier. Luther recognized three broad areas of vocation, *Nährstand*, agriculture and all that ministers to the body, *Lehrstand*, education, the work of ministry, and all that serves the mind and spirit, and *Nehrstand*, government in all its functions including the military. But Luther was strong against the idea of a crusade, and equally strong against the Peasants' Revolt.

Luther was uneasy. Zwingli and Calvin, more theocratic, held not merely by the Just War but by the holy war. Zwingli had at one time been close to Grebel, but moved far away from his theology of suffering love, advocated war in defence of the New Israel, and died fighting: Luther saw his death as a judgement for taking the sword as a minister of the gospel. Calvin was still more militantly theocratic, seeing the state as a positive instrument in support of true religion. His associate Theodore Beza justified violent rebellion; society is a covenant between God, the ruler and the people, and if the ruler violates it the people under God may use violence to vindicate it. The result of these views, and similar Catholic views, was the wars of religion, fought with great bitterness and many atrocities, which wrung from Chanon (who knew his Thucydides) the appalling judgement, 'Only Christians are permitted to rage against each other with every variety of inhumanity provided it be for the advancement of one party and the detriment of another. Those who are moderate are held suspect.'

Cromwell is the great seventeenth-century example of Christianity in arms. The Puritans had wrestled with the doctrine of the Just War, but that allowed no formula for rebellion against the prince. They rationalized this by opposing not the king but his advisers, the Malignants; but the king identified himself with the Malignants' cause. Another rationalization vested power in a balance of king, lords and commons, but that gave the commons no more right to check the king than the king the commons. Yet another suggested that a prince who behaved tyrannically ceased to hold legitimate authority.

Oliver Cromwell was impatient with such fine-spun arguments; they were 'fleshly reasonings'. He looked to divine authority. 'Let us look into providences; surely they mean somewhat. They hang so together; they being so constant, so clear and unclouded.' The determination of a holy war lay not with prince nor people but with God. So Edmund Calamy in 1643 appealed to the Old Testament where the priests sounded the trumpets for war. 'And certainly, if this were the way of God in the Old Testament, certainly much more in a Cause as this, in which Cause Religion is entwin'd and indeed so interlac'd, that Religion and this Cause, they are like Hippocrates his twins, they must live and die together.' So Cromwell halted at St Abb's Head to sing the sixty-eighth psalm ('Let God arise and let his enemies be scattered'), and described his victory against the odds as 'an unspeakable mercy'. So John Redingstone in 1649 declared, 'The Saints receive their commission from the great King, King of kings, to have a two edged sword in their hands, to execute judgement upon the Heathen and punishment upon the people . . . Hence then we see what a type of Holy Writ lies upon our Parliament and Arms, to execute judgement upon the King and his wicked Adherents.' Cromwell is reported as claiming that 'there are great occasions in which some men are called to great services in the doing of which they are excused from the common rule of morality' and adducing the Old Testament in support. There is here no finely calculated defence of the Just War; there is a certainty of divine commission for a holy war.

THE MODERN ERA

For two centuries and a half officially Christian nations fought war after war. Up till 1815 war marched about Europe. Then for a century Europe enjoyed relative peace, but war was exported all over the world. The churches, apart from a small minority, held to the doctrine of the Just War. But wars were not examined for their justice so much as accepted as part of the warp and woof of life. It was for most unthinkable that nationalism and Christianity should pull in different directions, but if they did nationalism won. The situation was of course theologically impossible, and when. a new and unprecedentedly devastating war shattered Europe in 1914 a minor English poet and man of letters, J. C. Squire, satirized it:

> God heard the embattled nations sing and shout
> 'Gott strafe England!' and 'God save the King!'
> God this, God that, and God the other thing –
> 'Good God!' said God, 'I've got my work cut out.'

The satire was called for. The Bishop of London, Winnington-Ingram, said, 'Kill Germans – to kill them, not for the sake of killing, but to save the world, to kill the good as well as the bad, to kill the young men as well as the old, to kill those who have shewn kindness to our wounded as well as those fiends who crucified the Canadian Sergeant.' This, if it was anything, was the holy war again. The only trouble was that both sides were supposed to be Christian and Christians on each side were fighting their own holy war.

Quakers had maintained a different witness. One had gone on a personal mission to the Czar to tell him that war was wrong. 'I have a message for you from Almighty God, Sire.' 'I am always delighted to receive a communication from the Almighty', said the Czar. He listened courteously, and the result was the Hague Peace Conference. Tolstoy in Russia had already, wrestling with his Crimea experiences, come to the view that Christianity must lead to absolute pacifism. In Germany his disciple Bertha von Suttner wrote the pacifist novel *Die Waffen Nieder* in 1889; this in turn led the Swedish chemist Alfred Nobel, who fondly imagined that his development of explosives had made war too horrible to practise, to found his peace prize. In 1907 Catholics, Protestants and Jews jointly petitioned the Second Hague Peace Conference for the cessation of the arms race. In 1914 as the clouds of war darkened over Europe a German Lutheran, chaplain to the Kaiser, Friedrich Siegmund-Schulze, and an English Quaker, Henry Hodgkin, shook hands on Cologne railway station and said, 'We are one in Christ and can never be at war.' In December 1914 Hodgkin, with the Presbyterian Richard Roberts, and about 130 others, met in Cambridge and formed the Fellowship of Reconciliation, which later became international, and remains the principal interdenominational Christian pacifist movement. The basis was expressed in five points.

1 That Love, as revealed and interpreted in the life and death of Jesus Christ, involves more than we have yet seen, that it is the only power by which evil can be overcome and the only sufficient basis of human society.

2 That, in order to establish a world-order based on Love, it is incumbent upon those who believe in this principle to accept it fully, both for themselves and in relation to others, and to take the risks involved in doing so in a world which does not as yet accept it.

3 That, therefore, as Christians, we are forbidden to wage war, and that our loyalty to our country, to humanity, to the Church Universal, and to Jesus Christ our Lord and Master, calls us instead to a life-service for the enthronement of Love in personal, commercial and national life.

4 That the Power, Wisdom and Love of God stretch far beyond the limits of our present experience, and that He is ever waiting to break forth into human life in new and larger ways.

5 That since God manifests Himself in the world through men and women, we offer ourselves to Him for His redemptive purpose, to be used by Him in whatever way He may reveal to us.

Between the wars the pacifist understanding of Christianity became more widespread, though it did not touch more than a tiny fraction of the main branches of Christianity, Catholic, Orthodox, Lutheran and Reformed. It was strongest in the English-speaking countries, and among the nonconformist sects. The excesses of Nazism led many to oppose Hitler's ambitions by violence, and to see opposition to German aggression as falling clearly within the scope of the Just War, and indeed as a kind of crusade 'in defence of democracy'. In America Reinhold Niebuhr, revolted by a pacifism which was sentimental and not deeply rooted in the theology of the cross, was particularly influential in arguing that Christians live in an imperfect world, and are imperfect themselves and cannot live out the perfect way of Jesus. But since the Second World War Christians have been increasingly uneasy. Among the Catholic hierarchy, for example, Cardinal Ottaviani has pronounced *bellum omnino interdicendum*, war is to be completely outlawed. In his message on 18 October 1975 Pope Paul VI spoke on the 'implacable theme of peace', and declared that arms and wars are to be excluded from civilization's programmes, and that the teaching of the Sermon on the Mount is no longer a simple, ingenuous and dangerous utopia, but the new Law of mankind.

The doctrine of the Just War has largely broken down in face of the immensely destructive weapons available and incompatible with the limitations traditionally imposed by that doctrine, though Paul Ramsey, an American theologian, has reaffirmed it in two major works. Ramsey rejects pacifism as unrealistic and massive deterrence as un-Christian, and calls for what he terms a 'just war statecraft'. He makes much of the ethical distinctions between murder and killing in war, and between murderousness and legitimate deterrence. Ultimately he believes that violence may be the only way of exercising Christian love towards the neighbour to defend him against oppression. Probably the majority of Christians now, however, think of war not as just but as justified. They do not see how the Nazis could have been checked except by war, and see the war against the Nazis as justified because it ended the threat of Nazi world-domination. They see the same sort of threat today (many Russian and Chinese Christians see it as posed by the USA and many American Christians as posed by Russia and China), and if it became excessive would think it justified to resist it by war precisely because they can see no other effective means of resistance. So too most Christians would not think of nuclear deterrents as just, but regard them as justified, because there has not been a third world war, and because they are uncertain of what might happen if they were removed.

The uneasiness is well seen in the World Council of Churches document *Violence, Nonviolence and the Struggle for Social Justice* (1973) where there are three major assertions. First, that non-violence is the only Christian method. Second, that violence is permitted in extreme circumstances. There must be just cause, the exhaustion of other possibilities, a reasonable expectation of attaining the desired ends, just methods and a positive concept of the ensuing order. Third, that those in situations of violence cannot help but react with violence; non-violence means opting out; the Christian must stay in, humanize the means of conflict, and build just structures for peace. Some types of violence are ruled out altogether: conquest, the oppression of class or race, torture, the taking of hostages, and the killing of non-combatants. One wonders how seriously some of this is meant; the theme is admittedly revolution, not war, but if the success of the revolution depended on extracting information from one opponent by torture, or the incidental death of a single non-combatant, would those Christians who have already accepted that in the last resort the end justifies the means refuse these further steps? This is a deeply unsatisfactory document. None the less in its agonized reappraisal there is a great change from the unthinking acceptance of violence by most church leaders in 1914 or even 1939.

In this change there have been three major factors. First, the development of nuclear bombs and other weapons of indiscriminate destruction have made it clear that no future war will ever conform to the principles laid down by the doctors of the Church as defining the Just War. Secondly, the work of concerned and committed scholars has established beyond much challenge that (as a Church of England Commission put it in 1974) the way of Jesus and the New Testament is pacifist, though it remains an open question whether we are called to follow this in the twentieth century. Thirdly, the practical experience of a number of exponents of religion in politics, Gandhi, a non-Christian much influenced by Christianity, in India, Candedo Rondon and Helder Camara in Brazil, Martin Luther King in the U.S.A., Danilo Dolci in Sicily, to name but a few, has shown that there are alternative methods, which seem closer to the way of Jesus, of effectively resisting violence and challenging tyranny without recourse to violence.

SUMMARY

Christianity has shown three principal attitudes to war, three historic positions. Pacifism was the dominant position up to the reign of Constantine, and has been viewed with increasing sympathy in the twentieth century. But within this position there are many variations. Thus John Howard Yoder in his remarkable *Nevertheless* analysed the varieties of religious pacifism with a subtlety and scholarship not marred by his somewhat journalistic titles. Each section is headed 'The Pacifism of – ': Christian Cosmopolitanism; the Honest Study of Cases; Absolute Principle; Programmatic Political Alternatives; Nonviolent Social Change; Prophetic Protest; Proclamation; Utopian Purism; the Virtuous Minority; the Categorical Imperative; Absolute Conscience; Redemptive Personalism; Cultic Law; Cultural Isolation; Consistent Nonconformity (The Non-Pacifist Nonresistance of the Mennonite 'Second Wind'); the Eschatological Parenthesis; Anarchism; Self-negation; the Very Long View; Instrumental Suffering; the Imitation of Jesus; Self-discipline; the Specific Situation; the Messianic Community.

It would be possible to compile an even more complex list of non-pacifist positions. Two have predominated. In the fourth century Christian theologians took over from Cicero the doctrine of the Just War, that is the position that Christians may legitimately take part in war provided that it is declared by a properly constituted authority and that certain ethical conditions are maintained in the conduct of the war. In the Middle Ages the idea of the crusade emerged, partly to save Christendom from internecine fighting; it was closely linked to the Old Testament concept of the holy war. At all times, however, there as been uneasiness about ministers of the Christian gospel, priests, monks and nuns, themselves participating in the fighting, though they have generally been prepared to bless others. For the majority of the Christian laity at all times, the claims of their nation have been paramount, even when called to fight against their fellow-Christians; often they have gone to war because they could see no realistic alternative. The historic association of the Christian faith with nations of commercial enterprise, imperialistic expansion and technological advancement has meant that Christian peoples, although their faith is one of the most pacifistic in its origins, have a record of military activity second to none.

FOR FURTHER READING

Bainton, R. H., *Christian Attitudes toward War and Peace.* Nashville, Abingdon, 1960.

Bethune-Baker, J. F., *The Influence of Christianity on War.* Cambridge, 1888.

Cadoux, C. J., *The Early Christian Attitude to War.* Swarthmore Press, 1919.

Cadoux, C. J., *The Early Church and the World.* T. and T. Clark 1925.

Ferguson, J., *The Politics of Love.* James Clarke n.d. (1973).

Harnack, A., *Militia Christi.* Tübingen, J. C. B. More (Paul Siebeck), 1905.

Heering, G. J., *The Fall of Christianity*, Eng. tr. Allen and Unwin, 1930.

Hengel, M., *Was Jesus a Revolutionist?*, Eng. tr. Philadelphia, Fortress Press, 1971.

MacGregor, G. H. C., *The New Testament Basis of Pacifism.* James Clarke, 1936.

Niebuhr, R., *Christianity and Power Politics.* Scribner, 1940.

Nuttall, G. F., *Christian Pacifism in History.* Blackwell, 1958.

Ramsey, P., *War and the Christian Conscience.* Durham, N. C., Duke University Press, 1961.

Ramsey, P., *The Just War.* Scribner, 1968.

CHRISTIANITY

Regout, R., *La doctrine de la guerre juste de Saint Augustin à nos jours.* Paris, 1935.

Russell, F. H., *The Just War in the Middle Ages.* Cambridge University Press, 1975.

Scott-Craig, T. S. K., *Christian Attitudes to War and Peace.* Edinburgh, Oliver & Boyd, 1938.

Stratmann, F. M., *Weltkirke und Weltfriede.* Augsburg, 1924.

Sturzo, L., *Church and State*, Eng. tr. Bles, 1939.

Tooke, Joan D., *The Just War in Aquinas and Grotius.* SPCK, 1965.

Vanderpol, A., *La Doctrine Scholastique du Droit de Guerre.* Paris, 1930.

Windass, S., *Christianity versus Violence: A Social and Historical Study of War and Christianity.* Sheed and Ward, 1964.

Yoder, J. H., *Nevertheless.* Scottsdale, Pa., Herald Press, 1971.

Zampaglione, G., *The Idea of Peace in Antiquity*, Eng. tr. Notre Dame, University of Notre Dame Press, 1973.

Chapter 8

ISLAM

THE PROPHET

Muhammad, the Prophet of Islam, was born about the year 570 C.E. in Mecca in Arabia. He was taken into the employment of a wealthy widow named Khadija, whom he subsequently married. At the age of forty he had a religious experience which led him to accept the calling of a prophet, and particularly to challenge on the one hand polytheism and superstition, and on the other social injustice and the irresponsible use of economic power. He acquired something of a following, beginning with Khadija, and including his successor, Abu Bakr; his followers for the most part were middle-class, rather than from the dispossessors or the dispossessed.

His challenge to entrenched interests led to opposition. He was for a time protected by an influential uncle Abu Talib, but was eventually forced to leave Mecca in the famous *Hijra* ('migration') in 622, and with his followers emigrated to Medina (Yathrib). Here he established the new community of Islam, or *umma*, a concept of great importance for Islam. The Constitution of Medina laid down the principles of the new community; it is 'a charter of Muhammad the prophet amongst the believers and the Muslims of the Quraysh and of Yathrib, and amongst those who follow them and attach themselves to them and fight along with them. There is one community over against mankind.' Here is the first overt expression of militancy as one of the marks of the new community. At the same time some of the later Pillars of the Faith were introduced, especially the affirmation that 'There is no god but God, and Muhammad is the

124

Apostle of God', together with prayer, fasting, and monetary contribution to the needs of the faithful.

The Prophet's faith centred on the One God. The one mortal sin was to deny that singleness, that unity. Anyone who says that 'There is no god but God' with sincerity enters Paradise, no matter what other sins he commits.

> He is God alone, God the Undivided
> He does not beget and He is not begotten
> There is none coequal with Him.

Surah 112

To affirm this is said to result in shedding one's sins like leaves in autumn. God is the Self-Existent, He is True Reality. He is omnipotent and omniscient. He is the Creator and the Giver of Life. His will is absolute; He guides and He leads astray; He overthrows and He builds; He is the Doer of what He intends. (The seeming contradiction between the absolute power of God, with the implication of predestination, and man's responsibility for his own misdeeds created a problem for later theologians.) God reveals his will (but not his essential Being) in the revelations to the Prophet known as *surahs*, and gathered in the Qur'an.

God's will is absolute, and man's response is *Islam*, or submission. Man's characteristic status is as the *'abd*, the slave or servant of God. But there is here an anomaly. During the Medina period there also emerged the concept of the *jihad*. The word means effort or striving, but we can understand something of its movement or meaning if we compare the English words 'striving' and 'strife'. Primarily then it is a striving in the way of God, it is effort for the community of Islam and its theocratic way. It is the pursuit of the worship of the One God by whatever means; it is just here that the subjection of all ethical principles to the one great theological affirmation is vital for the understanding of the development of Islam.

There is here an interaction of theological principle and historical accident. It happened that intertribal raiding was a major activity among the Arabs at this period. Muhammad had the option of seeking to abolish the practice, letting it be, or controlling it. There was nothing in his vision which pointed to the first; the second might be disruptive of the new community; he took the third way. He himself fostered raids on the caravans plying to and from Mecca; he was deeply persuaded that business interests in Mecca were at the root of the social evils of the day, and were standing in the way of religious reform. What he banned was intertribal raiding within the *umma* of Islam. It followed that the tribes round about had *de facto* the choice between accepting Islam and suffering the increasing military power of Medina. As tribes acceded to the faith raiding moved further afield, even four or five hundred miles away. A notable success was the submission of Mecca in 630, giving the new faith a centre of pilgrimage, and a fifth Pillar. What happened in this period was that war became a means of spreading the faith, at first indirectly, since those who accepted the faith were protected against war, but increasingly directly. War similarly came to play an increasingly effective part in the striving of the faithful for their faith, and the *jihad* came more and more to be identified with a Holy War undertaken for the faith.

THE JIHAD

Muhammad died in 632. In the next thirty years the community was led by four successors or caliphs. The Prophet's death led to widespread defections, and the two years' rule of Abu Bakr was largely spent in re-establishing the *umma* and reasserting the political unity of the Arabs. The next twenty-two years, under the caliphates of Umar and Uthman, saw a dramatic growth in the geographical power of Islam, which spread into Mesopotamia, Syria and Egypt. Partly this was the result of natural causes; the ending of intertribal warfare within the *umma*, and the prohibition of female infanticide led to overpopulation and consequent pressure to expand into the surrounding territories, especially as they offered fertility, and economic resources not found in Arabia. At the same time the passion for the glory of God represented by the *jihad* fostered military expansion.

It is important to reiterate what the military side of the *jihad* achieved. It offered to the tribes round about the choice between free accession to the *umma* of Islam, and military subjugation. It led to the substantial enlargement of the *dar-al-Islam*, the territory under the political control of Islam. But it did not of itself force those of other convictions into the faith, and the Christians of Syria and the Near East generally, if they remained firm in their own faith, were in fact unmolested and might rise to positions of considerable responsibility. There were indeed numerous conversions from Christianity to Islam in Syria and Egypt at this period, but preachment and persuasion also form an integral part of the effort for Islam, and the Qur'an opposes the use of violence as a means of conversion.

In 661 the Medina caliphate ended in blood, and power till the middle of the following century shifted to the Umayyad caliphs of Damascus. This again was a period of the immense enlargement of the *dar-al-Islam*. The armies of Islam swept in one direction along the North African coast, and across to Sicily and Spain, and were checked from further advances into Europe only by their defeat at Poitiers in 732. The crossing into Europe was explicitly justified as part of the *jihad*. But Muslim rule in Spain was one of tolerance, not of persecution. Jews who had suffered Christian intolerance found a refreshing and relieving contrast in the attitude of Islam, and non-Muslims, whether Jews or Christians, who retained their religious faith while offering political loyalty to the new regime were known as Mozarabs or near-Arabs. T. W. Arnold actually said of the Muslims in Spain that 'it was probably in a great measure their tolerant attitude towards the Christian religion that facilitated their rapid acquisition of the country'. In the same period Muslim armies under Muhammad ibn Qasim reached northern India, and established a bridgehead of Muslim power in Sind and the Punjab. Somewhat as the Jews had welcomed the armies of Islam in Spain as a relief from Christian persecution, so the Buddhists welcomed them to north India, as a relief from Hindu persecution. Qasim tolerated Hindus and Buddhists alike; they had their sacred scriptures; they were people of a book, and entitled to protection. Qasim is a characteristic combination of military aggression and religious tolerance.

THE PROBLEM OF DEFEAT

The Prophet was not afraid to use military force, and there are two important instances in the Qur'an, one of success and one of failure. In the second year of the *hijra* a small Muslim army met a Meccan force which greatly outnumbered them at Badr, and roundly defeated them. It appears that the Muslims deliberately turned aside from caravan-raiding to confront the larger force, confident in the support of God for the righteous.

> Already there has been for you a sign
> in the two armies that met.
> One was fighting in the cause of God,
> the other was resisting in unbelief.
> These saw with their own eyes twice their own number,
> but God strengthens with his help whom he wills.
> Surely is that a warning for those who open their eyes.
>
> Qur'an 3, 11

But in the following year the Meccans returned with a larger force, and defeated the Muslims at Uhud. This raised a problem for the faithful. Why had God allowed this defeat?

Four answers were canvassed. One was that the defeat was a merited retribution for over-confidence. Still, not all Muslims were guilty of this, and it would be monstrous to suggest that those who died in battle were more guilty of it than others. The Qur'an is strong to insist that though suffering may in some cases be a punishment for sin, it is not always so (24, 60; 48, 17). So the second answer canvassed is that suffering is a test of faith. So is prosperity.

> Every soul tastes of death,
> and we test you with evil and with good as a trial,
> and to us you will return. (21, 36)

The third view was that defeat was sent to reinforce the sense of dependence on God. Finally if none of these proved convincing the Muslim rested in the inscrutable providence of God.

No part of the matter is yours,
whether he turns towards them, or whether he punishes
    them;
for truly they do dark deeds.
To God belongs everything in the heavens and in the earth:
he forgives whom he wills,
he punishes whom he wills,
and God is forgiving, compassionate. (3, 123)

The problem of reconciling this absolute dependence upon God with the relativities of military politics is seen also in relation to the treaty of Hudaibiya. Were the Muslims right to make a treaty with God's enemies, with superstitious pagans? Should they rather have descended on Mecca as the instruments of God's wrath? The answer of the Qur'an is a rationalization.

And if there had not been believing men and believing women,
whom you did not know that you were trampling down,
and on whose account you would have incurred guilt unwittingly –
that God may bring into his mercy whom he wills –
if they had been separated out,
then we would certainly have punished those of them
who resisted God with a heavy punishment. (48, 256)

THE BROTHERHOOD

In Muslim thought man is always a member of society, and thought of in relation to the community. This is especially true of the brotherhood of Islam (*umma*), which the Prophet compared to 'a single hand, like a compact wall whose bricks support each other'. But although man is a social animal he is not by nature socially righteous. 'Men are the enemies of one another' (Qur'an 20, 121). So society takes the form of the state, with authority vested (in the Muslim state) in the person of the caliph or imam.

We uphold the prayer for the welfare of the imams of the Muslims and the confession of their imamate; and we maintain the error of those who approve of the uprising against them whenever it appeared that they have abandoned the right; and we believe in the denial of an armed uprising against them and abstinence from fighting in civil war.

Al-Ash'ari *Kitab al-Ibana*

So internal violence was strictly forbidden even against tyrannous use of authority. Din ibn Jama'a (d. 1333 C.E.) actually affirmed that if in the absence of an imam someone usurped power, his authority became binding, and the duty of the Muslim was obedience, no matter how unjust the usurper. The maintenance of Muslim unity was primary.

There is some debate as to whether the Islamic state was national or universal. Pressures of the actual situation compelled Muhammad and his successors to introduce legislation which was linked to Arab traditions, but there is no real doubt that the essential view of the Qur'an is of a single worldwide community: one God, one mankind, one law, one ruler. 'If there were two gods, the universe would be ruined' (Qur'an 21, 23).

THE PHILOSOPHY OF THE JIHAD

The chief instrument for the spreading of Islam and for the establishment of a world-state was the *jihad*. The word means 'striving', and not necessarily war. There is a *jihad* of preaching and persuasion; one traditional saying has it that the monasticism of Islam is the *jihad*. The Muslim jurists in fact distinguished four different types of *jihad*, performed with heart, tongue, hands and sword. The first is exercised by the individual in his personal fight against evil. The second and third are largely exercised in support of the right and correction of the wrong. The fourth means war against unbelievers and enemies of the faith. It is part of the obligation of the faithful to offer their wealth and lives in this war (Qur'an 61, 11).

Muslim expansion was halted at Tours in the west and at the frontiers of India in the east. The world was not established as a single theocratic state. It was divided between *dar-al-Islam*, the territory of Islam, and *dar al-harb*, the territory of war. The first comprised Muslims, with full citizenship, and members of other religious faiths, who were allowed partial rights and granted toleration, provided that they acceded to Muslim rule and paid their taxes. The second was the realm of infidels or unbelievers. Between these two territories a state of war exists. There may be periods during which the *jihad* is in suspense, but they are temporary only, and theoretically should not last more than ten years. In practice, however, most Muslims accept the suspension of the *jihad* as normalcy, and Ibn Khaldun saw it as the passage from militarism to civilization.

It is an important aspect of the *jihad* that it maintained and encouraged the traditional belligerence of the Arabs, which, Ibn Khaldun maintained, was responsible for courage, self-reliance, and tribal unity, while ending the internecine strife between the tribes. Within the brotherhood of Islam war was strictly outlawed. Belligerence was diverted against the unbeliever. The doctrine of the *jihad* was in its own way the definition of a just war, directed against polytheists, apostates and enemies of Islam, and positively towards the establishment of the universal theocratic state.

From time to time attempts were made to establish the *jihad* among the pillars of Islam, and indeed the Kharijis do so include it. They insist that since the Prophet spent most of his life in war, the faithful should follow his example, that the Islamic state should be permanently organized for war, and that heretics should be forcibly converted or put to the sword. They stood on a tradition which ascribed to the Prophet the words, 'My fate is under the shadow of my spear.' They were merciless in fighting, killing non-combatants and prisoners of war without ruth; their own lives were austere and self-disciplined.

In general, however, the *jihad* is not among the five pillars of the Faith. This is because the pillars, affirmation (*shahada*), prayer (*salat*), almsgiving (*zakat*), fasting (*saum*) and pilgrimage (*hajj*), are obligatory on individuals. It is almost universally agreed among Muslim jurists that the *jihad* is a collective obligation of Islam (*fard al-kifaya*); it is laid on the community, not on the individual. Indeed it is explicitly stated in the Qur'an that not all believers should actively participate in war (9, 123). Similarly the *jihad* is the responsibility of the state; an individual believer cannot wage his own *jihad*. But participation in the communal duty leading to death in Allah's path is a sure guarantee of immediate paradise and exemption from trial on the Day of Judgement. 'Count not those who are killed in the path of Allah as dead; they are alive with their Lord' (Qur'an 3, 163), or, as one traditional saying puts it, 'There are one hundred stages in Paradise that are provided by Allah for those who fight in His path.' In one story Muhammad comforts a mother who has lost her son in battle: 'Your son is in the higher Paradise!' Such martyrs of the faith are not ceremonially prepared for burial, but buried on the battlefield.

Ibn Khaldun (1332–1406 C.E.) has an important analysis of war. War is not an accidental calamity or a disease; its roots are in the nature of man, selfish, jealous, angry, revengeful. Wars are of four kinds: tribal wars, feuds and raids, the *jihad*, wars against rebels and dissenters. The first two are wars of disobedience and unjustified, the second two are wars of obedience and justified. Ibn Khaldun is insistent that military victory depends on two factors, military preparedness and spiritual insight; the latter includes the dedication of the commander, the morale of the army, the use of psychological warfare, and informed and inspired decision-making.

Muslim jurists submitted the *jihad* itself to close analysis.

(a) The *jihad* against polytheists. The Qur'an lays upon the faithful the injunction to 'fight the polytheists whenever you may find them' (9, 5), to 'fight those of the polytheists who are near you, and let them feel your severity' (9, 124), to 'strike off the heads of misbelievers in a total massacre' (47, 4). One tradition attributes to the Prophet the words, 'I am ordered to fight polytheists until they say "There is no god but Allah".'

(b) The *jihad* against believers. This was subdivided by al-Mawardi:

    (i)   The *jihad* against apostasy. If apostates joined the *dar-al-harb*, they became subject to the *jihad*. The outstanding historical example of this was the secession of the Arab tribes after Muhammad's death. Abu Bakr gave them solemn warning, after which they were harried with fire and the sword.

    (ii) The *jihad* against dissension. A good historical example is the disagreement between the Kharijis and the Caliph 'Ali.

They were given the option of continuing to pray in the mosque, peaceful relations with the caliph, and residence in the dar al-Islam. They rejected this and continued to oppose the caliph, who overwhelmed them in the battle of al-Nahruwan (658 C.E.).

(iii) The *jihad* against bandits. Here there is a Qur'anic injunction:

The punishment of those who combat Allah and His Apostle, and go about to commit disorders on the earth: they should be executed or crucified or have their hands and their feet cut off or be banished from the land. This shall be a disgrace for them in the world, and in the next they shall have great torment (5, 37).

(c) The *jihad* against the People of a Book. Jews, Christians, and (less certainly) Zoroastrians were regarded as different from polytheists. They believed in Allah, and they possessed Holy Scriptures. But they rejected Allah's Apostle. Therefore they should be given a choice. They might embrace Islam and become full citizens. They might retain their present beliefs on condition that they accepted the authority of the imam and paid their taxes; in which event they were tolerated and granted partial rights. If they rejected both these, they became subject to the *jihad*.

(d) The *ribat*, or strengthening of the frontiers, was brought within the *jihad* by some jurists. Its scriptural justification lies in the words: 'Prepare against them what force and companies of horse you can, to make the enemies of God, and your enemies, and others beside them, in a state of dread' (Qur'an 8, 62). On the whole the *ribat* was interpreted defensively. 'Abd-Allah ibn 'Umar said that the *jihad* was for combating unbelievers, the *ribat* for protecting believers. Ibn Hudhayl in the twelfth century wrote a treatise on the *jihad*, devoting a whole chapter to the *ribat*, and stressing the importance of the defence of Spain against the unbelievers. One tradition attributes to the Prophet Muhammad the statement that the *ribat* was more important than the *jihad*, and that one night spent on a *ribat* was worth a thousand spent in prayer.

There were certain rules about participation in a *jihad*. The participants must be believers (though some jurists disagreed, and Muhammad's own practice seems to have varied), adult, male (except in defence against surprise attack and in indirect support for the war), sound in mind and body ('Allah will not burden any soul beyond its power' – Qur'an 2, 286), free, economically independent, acting with parental support, and endowed with good intentions. They must follow the injunction, 'Obey Allah and the Apostle and those in authority among you' (Qur'an 4, 62). They must behave honourably and keep their word. They must not retreat except as a last resort.

The caliph or imam was responsible for declaration of war. There should always be an invitation to accede to Islam, and it was normal to allow three days' grace before the actual war. In early days the army was quite small; the total force at al-Qadisiyya in 637 C.E. is said to have totalled 12,000, being outnumbered by the Persians by ten to one. The organization was straightforwardly in five units, vanguard, centre, two wings and rearguard. The army were professional fighters and kept away from agriculture. Under the Umayyads military conscription was introduced, and the organization of the army adopted Byzantine methods. The 'Abbasids kept a clear distinction between the army regulars and volunteers recruited for particular purposes on temporary pay. Before battle Qur'anic passages relating to the *jihad* would be read as an exhortation, often together with war-poems.

The jurists laid down certain rules of war, though they offered differing judgements. They agreed that non-combatants should be spared unless they were indirectly helping the enemy cause; at the battle of Hunayn a centenarian named Durayyd ibn al-Simma was killed in the Prophet's presence for giving advice to the enemy. Some jurists held that all which the participants in the *jihad* could not control should be destroyed; others that inanimate objects and crops should be destroyed but animals should be spared; others that everything should go except flocks and beehives. Destruction and poisoning of water supply were permitted. Spoils belonged to participants only, one-fifth going to the state.

In the early days there was no fighting in the sacred months

134

(Qur'an 9, 5), but later more stress was placed on another Qur'anic injunction:

> They will ask you about war in the sacred month. Say: to war at that time is bad, but to turn aside from the cause of Allah, and to have no faith in Him, and in the sacred Temple, and to drive out its people, is worse in the sight of Allah (12, 214).

An example of a more recent *jihad* will be found in the career of Usuman dan Fodio, leader of the Fulani in what is now Nigeria. He began a *jihad* against the Hausa rulers, conquering Gobir in 1804. He took the title Commander of the Faithful, and set up an Islamic state. Some Hausa Muslims protested that he was in fact fighting illegally against the faithful. His highly articulate son, Sultan Bello, denied this: 'Though they called themselves Muslims and made the confession of faith and prayed and fasted, yet with these acts they joined that which none but heathens would do, such as sacrifices to stones and trees.' Bello insisted that this was a true *jihad*; it was a defence against aggression, a conversion of the heathen and a strengthening of Islam. The *jihad* pushed further south and won over for Islam many pagan tribes, creating an integrated Muslim society over most of northern Nigeria.

Similarly the Turkish action under Mustafa Kemal Ataturk to remove Greek and Allied forces from Anatolia after the first World War was seen as a *jihad*, and on 19 September 1921 Mustafa Kemal was formally accorded the rank of Ghazi, given only to those who have participated in a *jihad*.

ARBITRATION

One important aspect of Muslim law lies in the concept of arbitration. It has a Qur'anic basis:

> O you who believe! Obey Allah and obey the Apostle, and those among you invested with authority; and if you differ upon any matter, refer it to Allah and the Apostle, if you believe in Allah and in the last day. This is the best and fairest way of settlement. (4, 62)

Arbitration was a method of settling disputes within Islam to avoid the temptation of fighting among themselves. But Muhammad had submitted to arbitration a dispute with a Jewish tribe, Banu Qurayza, and this precedent led to the principle that arbitration was permitted between Muslim and non-Muslim communities in matters which did not involve the faith, arrangements to end fighting, for example. A well-known historical example of arbitration within Islam lay in the conflict between 'Ali, the fourth caliph, and Mu'awiya, governor of Syria. Mu'awiya ordered his soldiers to raise the Qur'an on their lances; he was appealing to its authority. Both leaders appointed arbitrators, who were required to give a judgement within a year. They met and agreed on their decision, to depose both and lay the matter open to popular election. But in the announcement one of them withdrew, and 'Ali was able to say that they had gone away from the principles of the Qur'an. Arbitration served a limited purpose, but had a value in checking internecine strife.

MUSLIM PACIFISM

It should be said that pacifism is not unknown in Islam. One sect, the Maziyariyya, dropped fasting from the pillars of the Faith, and the *jihad* altogether. This however is exceptional.

More frequent is the inclination to emphasize the spiritual aspect of the teaching of the *jihad*. This is especially strong among the Sufis. Thus al-Qushayri (d. 1074 C.E.) claimed that the basis of the *jihad* is weaning the Self from its habitual ways and directing it contrary to its desires. The *jihad* of ordinary people consists in fulfilling actions, the *jihad* of the elect lies in purifying the interior state. So too al-Jilani (d. 1166 C.E.) cites the Prophet as saying, 'We have returned from the lesser *jihad* to the greater *jihad*': that is that the conquest of the Self is a greater struggle than the conquest of external enemies.

So too the Ahmadiyya movement stresses the meaning of striving, or exertion. The spirit of the *jihad* 'enjoins on every Muslim to sacrifice his all for the protection of the weak and oppressed whether Muslims or not'. They emphasize the need for active resistance and not just prayer and meditation. The test of *jihad* lies in the willingness to suffer, not in the practice of warfare. They totally disown the concept of a *jihad* directed to the expansion of Islam. They accept that there may be a necessity of armed defence against aggression. But the essence of the *jihad* lies in an active concern for the oppressed.

One remarkable demonstration of Muslim pacifism took place among the Pathans of Northern India, a people with traditions of violence. 'Abdul Ghaffir Khan, 'the Gandhi of the frontier provinces', a puritan reformer, in 1930 persuaded the Pathans of the power of non-violence. Persecution, imprisonment and executions did not shake them: they persisted for years in the courageous commitment to non-violence. So the striving of Islam can turn to peace.

FOR FURTHER READING

ISLAM

Abu Zahra, Shaykh, *The Concept of War in Islam*. Cairo, Ministry of Waqfs, n.d.

Hague, S. A., *Islam's Contribution to the Peace of the World*. Lahore, Ahmadiya, n.d.

Khadduri, M., *War and Peace in the Law of Islam*. Baltimore, Md, Johns Hopkins, 1955.

Lewis, B., *The Arabs in History*. Hutchinson, 1950.

Rahman, F., *Islam*. Weidenfeld, 1966.

Smith, W. C., *Islam in Modern History*. Oxford, 1967.

Tendul Kar, D. G., *Abdul Ghaffar Khan: Faith is a Battle*. Bombay, Popular Prakasham, 1967.

Watt, W. M., *Muhammad, Prophet and Statesman*. Oxford, 1961.

Williams, J. A., *Themes of Islamic Civilization*. Berkeley, University of California, 1971.

Chapter 9

SIKHISM

'Sikhism', writes G. S. Sidhu, 'is an endeavour to create a union of all those who love God and serve humanity.' It is comprehensive, inclusive, tolerant. 'For the Sikh', he goes on, 'the whole humanity is a united family, a brotherhood under ONE GOD.' Sikhism is a way of life based on the unity of God, faith in the Guru, and love for all. It sprang from the seed left by the poet Kabir, who drew together Islam and Hinduism, which had warred together through the Middle Ages, into a common devotion to the one God who lies behind the many names, 'whether Allah or Rama'.

> He is One; there is no other.
> Rama, Khuda, Sakti, Siva are one.
> How can you hope to distinguish them?
> I hold firmly to the One Name.

Sikhism was born as a gospel of reconciliation. 'One of the central points in the Sikh faith', says a modern Sikh publicist, 'is the ideal of service to be given freely and disinterestedly to one's fellow men, no matter to what religion, race, political group, sex or sect they may belong.'

GURU NANAK

The founder of Sikhism, Guru Nanak (1469–1539), was born in a period of political corruption, and economic exploitation. Hindus

138

and Muslims hated one another, fought one another, exploited one another. Hindus were separated from one another by the caste system. Religion had become a combination of superstition and formal observance. Guru Nanak was born into a Hindu family living in the Punjab. But his search for truth was not sectarian and he would go with any who would search with him. His own call came in a vision of the Gates of Paradise opening, a drink being offered him, and the voice of God saying to him, 'I am with you. Go and repeat my Name and lead others to do the same.' His teaching centred on God, the True Name. It would not be too much to say that this was his teaching. Tradition says that he went on a series of pilgrimages to bring this teaching to different parts of the world, to Ceylon in the south, Mecca in the west, Russia and Turkestan in the north. Certainly he travelled, and may well have travelled beyond the Indian subcontinent. The Guru, though a man of peace, was not a pacifist, and declared, 'To fight and accept death for a righteous cause is the privilege of the brave and the truly religious.'

THE SUCCESSORS

The leaders who followed consolidated what Guru Nanak had begun. The second Guru, Angad, and the third, Amar Das, laid great stress on education, using the vernacular instead of concentrating on Sanskrit, and on equality. The fourth Guru, Ram Das, was responsible for the foundation of Amritsar as a major trading centre; the result of this was that the Sikh leader became a worldly potentate as well as a spiritual guide. Guru Arjan's period of leadership was a major turning-point. He was responsible for the compilation of the *Guru Granth Sahib*, the holy book of the Sikhs; he himself made his own contribution to spiritual devotion through his hymns. He also encouraged the Sikhs to trade in Turkish horses. This had four results: first, the breaking of superstition (there was a Hindu superstition against crossing the Indus); second, prosperity; third, the development of horse-riding and eventually of cavalry; fourth, dangerous contact with militant Islam. The great Jahangir wrote:

At Goindwral on the river Beas, lived a Hindu named Arjun in the garb of a saint. Many simple-minded Hindus and some ignorant and imbecile Muslims were attracted and ensnared by his ways. He was noised abroad as a spiritual teacher and people called him a prophet. Shoals of people came to him from all sides and made declarations of faith in him. This imposturous shop of his had been running briskly over three or four generations. For years it was coming to my mind either to abolish this emporium of falsehood or convert him to Islam.

Jahangir, regarding the Guru as a heretic and religious deceiver, had him arrested and tortured to death.

This persecution led the Sikhs to take military measures for self-protection. The sixth Guru, Har Gobind, was imprisoned for a time, but on his release organized cavalry and artillery defences. He had an armed bodyguard, saying, 'I wear two swords as symbols of spiritual and temporal authority. In the Guru's house religion and worldly enjoyment shall be combined – the cauldron to supply the poor and needy, and the scimitar to smite oppressors.' Three times they were attacked; three times they repelled the attack. But they were content to stem aggression from outside, and made no political or territorial claims themselves. Their fierce self-defence led to a period of relative peace under the seventh and eighth Gurus. But the ninth Guru, Tegh Bahadur, coincided with the rule of Aurangzeb at Delhi. Aurangzeb was a believer in forcible conversion. Some Brahmins from Kashmir appealed to the Guru to protect them. The Guru promised to make his witness even at the cost of his life. He went to Delhi and made his protest. Eventually he was given the choice of death or conversion, and chose death.

THE TENTH GURU

The tenth Guru, Gobind Singh, as a young man enjoyed wearing a uniform, and engaging in musket-practice and archery. It was a period of constant clashes with the tribes in the hills. His advisers protested against military involvement. 'You need peace. Our Guru's business is with the Sikhism of his country. War is the role of kings.' But the Guru insisted on meeting arms with arms, and developed a disciplined army of Sikhs. This was the famous Khalsa, the Army of

Salvation, marked by the Five Ks, *Kesh* (hair), *Kangha* (comb), *Kara* (bangle), *Kachla* (shorts), *Kirpan* (sword). Those who came for military service were welcomed and trained. When there was no fighting they maintained military discipline by hunting. But the thought of the enemy in the hills was uppermost in his mind. His mother charged him with provocative behaviour. The Guru answered, 'We cannot remain subject to such people. If they play the part of aggressors, I will show them what the Guru can do. The immortal God has sent me into the world to uproot evil and protect from tyranny the weak and oppressed.' His mother went away in tears; the Guru put on his armour.

So wars came, and as the Guru armed, he prayed.

> Eternal God, our shield, O Lord,
> our dagger, arrow, spear and sword.
> To us for our defence is given
> the timeless, deathless Lord of heaven;
> to us, All-steel's unconquered might;
> to us, All-time's resistless flight;
> and you, All-steel, in all will render
> valiant service as our Defender.

The details of the fighting do not here matter. But the Guru affirmed that those who died fighting for the cause went to paradise and enjoyed everlasting life. He called one of his sons Zorawar Singh, or Mighty Lion, in commemoration of the battle of Nadaun. He wrote of himself:

> I am the destroyer of the turbulent hillmen;
> they are idolaters, I am iconoclast.

His devotional writings concentrated on the Sword and on God as the Sword. God first fashioned the Sword, then the universe. God subdues enemies, as does the Sword; so God is the Sword, and the Sword is God. First remember the Sword, then meditate on Guru Nanak. So too the Guru encouraged the translation of the ancient martial epics, *The Ramayana* and *The Mahabharata*, and himself translated the praises of the heroic Chandi to encourage men in the virtues of war.

There was fighting too with Muslim armies. The Sikhs went through great privation, and a period of defeat, but managed to hold out. There are records of the Muslim view of the Sikh armies, a low rabble, but undoubtedly brave, depending on practical organization and efficient defence, and at the same time on the spiritual insight and authority of the Guru. His vision and persistence were remarkable: 'Having obtained the order of the God, my object is to increase and not diminish the numbers of my religion. It is by enduring hunger and hardships my Sikhs become strong and brave.' He wrote a famous address to the Muslim ruler Aurangzeb. It begins with a characteristic invocation to God:

O Thou perfect in miracles, eternal, beneficent, Bestower of grace, maintenance, salvation and mercy, Dispenser of bliss, pardoner, Saviour, Remitter of sins, dear to the heart, King of kings, Bestower of excellence, Director of the way, without colour and without equal, Lord, who givest heavenly bliss to him who has no property, no retinue, no army and no comforts. Distinct from the world, powerful, whose light is everywhere diffused, Thou bestowest gifts as if Thou wert present in person. Pure Cherisher, Bestower of favours, Thou art merciful, and Provider of sustenance in every land. Thou art Lord of every clime, the greatest of the great. Perfect in beauty, merciful, Master of knowledge, Support of the unhappy, Protector of the Faith, Fountain of eloquence, Searcher of hearts, Author of revelation, Appreciator of wisdom, Lord of intelligence, Diviner of secrets, Omnipresent God, Thou knowest the affairs of the world. Thou resolvest its difficulties, Thou art its greatest Organizer.

To Aurangzeb he declares roundly that he does not trust his word. He gives an account of his recent defeat, in which, hopelessly outnumbered, the Sikhs still dealt out destruction. 'When an affair passes beyond the realm of diplomacy, it is lawful to have recourse to the sword.' He calls himself the slave and servant of the King of kings, and challenges Aurangzeb to the same calling. 'You are monarch of the world, but religion is far from you.' He extols his own

defeat of the hillmen. 'Behold the power of the good and pure God who by means of one man killed hundreds of thousands.'
He ends:

> God bestows peace on him who heartily performs His service. How can an enemy lead astray him with whom the Guide of the way is pleased? Should tens of thousands proceed against such a one, the Creator will be his guardian. When you look to your army and wealth, I look to God's praises. You are proud of your empire, while I am proud of the kingdom of the immortal God. Do not be heedless; this caravanserai is for a few days only, people leave it at every moment. See the revolution which passes over every inhabitant and every house in this faithless world. You may be strong, but do not persecute the weak. Do not lay the axe to your kingdom. When God is a friend what can an enemy do even if he multiplies himself a hundredfold? If an enemy practise enmity a thousand times, he cannot, as long as God is a friend, injure even a hair of one's head.

The opening of *Vichitar Natak* shows Guru Gobind Singh's military mysticism.

> I bow with love and devotion to the Holy Sword.
> Assist me that I may complete this work.

> Thou art the Subduer of countries, the Destroyer of the armies of the wicked, in the battlefield Thou greatly adornest the brave.
> Thine arm is infrangible, thy brightness refulgent, Thy radiance and splendour dazzle like the sun.
> Thou bestowest happiness on the good, Thou terrifiest the evil, Thou scatterest sinners, I seek thy protection.
> Hail! hail to the Creator of the world, the Saviour of creation, my Cherisher, hail to Thee, O Sword!

> I bow to Him who holds the arrow in His hand; I bow to the Fearless one.
> I bow to the God of gods who is in the present and the future.

I bow to the Scimitar, the two-edged Sword, the Falchion, and the Dagger.

Thou, O God, hast ever one form; Thou art ever unchangeable.

I bow to the Holder of the mace
who diffused light through the fourteen worlds.

I bow to the Arrow and the Musket.

I bow to the Sword, spotless, fearless, and unbreakable.

I bow to the powerful Mace and lance
to which nothing is equal.

I bow to Him who holds the discus,
who is not made of the elements and who is terrible.

I bow to Him with the strong teeth.

I bow to Him who is supremely powerful.

I bow to the Arrow and the Cannon
which destroy the enemy.

I bow to the Sword and the Rapier
which destroy the evil.

I bow to all weapons which may be held.

I bow to all weapons which may be hurled.

Thou turnest men like me from blades of grass into mountains; there is no other Cherisher of the poor but Thou.

O God, do Thou Thyself pardon my errors; there is none who has erred like me.

The houses of those who have served Thee are all seen filled with wealth.

In this Kal age and at all times there is great confidence in the powerful arm of the Sword.

Alongside this we may place a couple of quatrains from the Guru's baptismal service.

Trained soldiers, powerful, irresistible, well armoured with coats of mail, crush their enemies;

Filled with high martial spirit they would put mountains to flight, themselves unshaken;

They would shatter their enemies, destroy rebels, crush the pride of furious elephants;

Yet without the favour of God, the Lord of wealth, they should
all depart at last and leave the world.

Countless very valiant heroes without hesitation face the
sword's edge,
Subdue countries, crush rebels, and the pride of furious
elephants,
Break powerful forts and without resistance conquer in every
direction –
But their efforts are useless; the Lord is the Commander of
them all; the suppliants are many while there is but one Giver.

AFTER THE GURUS

With Guru Gobind Singh the line of Gurus came to an end. This is
itself significant. But the tenth Guru had appointed the formidable
Banda Singh as commander of the Sikh armies. The visible
leadership was military, not spiritual. Banda Singh was an able
general, who sacked Sirhind and established a power which ran from
Lahore to Panipat. But the emperor turned to diplomacy, and
succeeded in dividing the Sikhs into two parties by promising no
forcible conversions and a grant to the Golden Temple at Amritsar if
the Sikhs would promise to fight for him instead of against him.
Banda Singh stood out against this. He was besieged in the castle of
Gurdas Nangal; his followers were put to the sword, and he himself
captured and, refusing conversion, tortured to death. Systematic
persecution followed. The slogan of the government was 'Kill, kill
and kill again.' There was an official proclamation:

1 No Hindu in the Punjab will grow hair or beard. Refusal to obey
this law will be punished with death.
2 Anyone giving information leading to the arrest of a Sikh will be
eligible for a reward of Rs 5; anyone helping to arrest a Sikh will
receive Rs 10; anyone who brings the head of a Sikh to the police
station will receive Rs 15; anyone who brings in a Sikh alive will
be recompensed with Rs 50. For greater services the reward
earned will be a Jagir.
3 To entertain a Sikh is considered a crime.

The Sikhs went into hiding, and there was a period of extreme privation. But changes weakened the central government, and the Sikhs began a campaign of effective guerrilla warfare, organizing themselves into two platoons, one of veterans and one of recruits. This was so successful that the government offered them a measure of independence under their own Nawab. But the government was not to be trusted, and a massacre at a festival at the Golden Temple was narrowly averted. The body of the Sikhs did not come, and only their leader, Mani Singh, was killed.

In the following year, 1738, Nadir Shah invaded India. This gave the Sikhs a respite to fortify their defences, and the opportunity for a vengeance which ill accorded with the precepts of their founder. Their cavalry made lightning raids, and even plundered the plunderers. 'Where do these long-haired barbarians come from?' asked Nadir. 'Destroy them and their homes.' 'Their homes are their horses' saddles', was the reply. Their success was not unmixed. Yahia Khan's forces defeated them in battle, and there was again bitter persecution. After his death there was a period of chaos, during which Jassa Singh was able to reform the Khalsa. Mir Mannun as governor of Lahore renewed the persecution, but the Sikhs fought back:

> We are the crop and Mannun a sickle,
> The more he cuts us, the more we grow,
> In every house and hut.

For a short period Jassa Singh actually occupied Lahore; the Golden Temple at Amritsar was restored. The governor of Lahore actually was driven to asking the invading armies of Ahmad Shah to destroy the Sikhs. In 1762 he met them at Kupp Rahira, and massacred 30,000, going on to destroy and pollute the Golden Temple.

But the Sikhs, like the early Romans, showed extraordinary resilience in defeat. Within three years they had re-established themselves, restored the power of the Khalsa and captured Lahore. They struck a coin with the inscription

> Prosperity, power and speedy success
> from Nanak to Guru Gobind Singh.

SIKHISM

The Khalsa met annually at Amritsar, and the chiefs offered their affirmation, 'The sacred *Granth* is at our side. Let us swear by our scripture to forget all internal disputes and to be counted.' Capital punishment was abolished, religious toleration was legally established, and works of charity were fostered. The leadership of Ranjit Singh consolidated Sikh power. He was a soldier of soldiers, an immensely respected authoritarian ruler, a man of great simplicity of life. Religious toleration was observed in principle and in practice; his leading minister was in fact a Muslim. He modernized the army, bringing in British and American officers to train them; it was now that the Sikhs came to be compared, as religious soldiery, with Cromwell's Ironsides. Ranjit Singh's ambitions to extend his power were however checked by the British, and when his death came in 1839 after a long reign, annexation could not be long delayed. The Sikhs were defeated by treachery and in 1846 a formal treaty of virtual subjugation was signed; five years later the annexation became a fact.

SIKHS IN THE TWENTIETH CENTURY

Early in the twentieth century Sikh military tradition was still reasserting itself in an unsuccessful attempt at violent revolution against the British. But gradually the spirit of resistance changed. The British authorities foolishly tried to break the spirit of the Sikhs by interfering with their religion. The influence of Mahatma Gandhi was now strong. In 1922 the Sikhs were refused permission to visit one of their temples. Every day 100 Sikhs marched up non-violently to defy the ban. Every day they were beaten unconscious without defending themselves or retaliating, or arrested and deported. The official report of the commission of inquiry on these events makes grim but powerful reading:

> The use of force was persisted in again and again with the result that several cases of skull injuries resulting in concussion of the brain and unconsciousness occurred. The Akalis took all these beatings without any resistance or any attempt at retaliation. Divesting ourselves of all political bias we consider that the excesses

committed reflect the greatest discredit on the Punjab Government. We have no hesitation whatever to come to the conclusion that the force used, judged from all aspects, was altogether excessive. We are constrained to observe that the arbitrary and lawless way in which violence was resorted to, was deliberate and in callous disregard of such humanity as even a Government is bound to show. Lastly, we cannot help expressing our profound admiration for the spirit of martyrdom and orderliness which animated the Akalis and for their unflinching adherence to the Gospel of non-violence and for the noble way in which they have vindicated themselves under circumstances of prolonged and unusual exasperation.

C. F. Andrews said that 'a new heroism, learnt through suffering, has arisen in the land. A new lesson in moral warfare has been taught to the world.' Unhappily, it was not to last. In the Second World War, while Christian Europe was involved in its own holocaust, the Sikhs returned to violent revolution. General Mohan Singh established the Indian National Army to throw the British out by violence, and casualties were heavy. With partition they became heavier still, and the Sikh community was scattered over the globe. The faith remains.

FOR FURTHER READING

Archer, J. C., *The Sikhs*. Princeton, 1946.

Latif, Mohammed, *History of the Panjab from the Remotest Antiquity to the Present Time*. Calcutta, 1891.

Macauliffe, M. A., *The Sikh Religion*, 6 vols. Oxford, 1909.

Malcolm, Sir John, *A Sketch of the Sikhs*. London, 1812.

Sidhu, G. S., *Introduction to Sikhism*. Sikh Missionary Society, 1973.

Singh, Avtar, *Ethics of the Sikhs*. Patiala, Punjab University, 1970.

Chapter 10

THE BAHA'I

The story of the Baha'i is particularly interesting, as the movement arose as a challenge to political and religious disunity.

THE BAB

Early in the nineteenth century there was a sense of religious expectation in Persia. Shaykh Ahmad of Ahsa (1753–1829) announced that he was preparing the way for him who must needs be made manifest in the fullness of time, and that nothing short of a new and independent Revelation as attested and foreshadowed by the Scriptures of Islam could revive the fortunes of that Faith which had fallen into decadence. After his death Seyyid Kazim of Resht (1789–1843) spoke of an imminent Advent, to take place after his own death. He would even say, 'Do you not desire me to depart in order that the Truth may be made manifest?' These two have been given the titles of the Two Preparatory Gates of God.

Shortly after, there appeared in Shiraz a young man named Mirza Ali Muhammad. He had been born on 20 October 1819, and married in 1841. In 1843 he had a mystic dream in which the Spirit of God possessed him with a glorious Revelation. But he was to be only a forerunner. On 23 May 1844 Muhammad Husayn was teaching about the expected Advent and identifying the token validating his appearance. Mirza Ali Muhammad pushed forward and said, 'See if these tokens be not in me.' Muhammad Husayn accepted this as a sign, and the young man as the Bab, or Gate; he himself is sometimes called the Gate of the Gate, or the Most Mighty Letter of the Book (that is, the Bab's book). The Bab was a man of great personal charm, simple and serene, but strong and independent at the same time. He had already acquired something of a reputation for piety, and for straight and generous business dealings. Now he struck out along new lines. He drew to himself nineteen apostles, and sent them out to spread the good news, not being afraid to make the comparison with Jesus and claim a higher destiny. Writings flowed freely from him, half a million lines and more, He declared, 'I am the Bab, the Gate of God', 'I am the Promised One, whose name you have for a thousand years invoked', 'I am the Primal Point from which have been generated all created things', 'I am the Countenance of God, whose splendour can never be obscured, the light of God whose radiance can never fade'. He proclaimed brotherly love, kindness to children, courtesy and dignity, sociability, hospitality, freedom from bigotry, friendliness to Christians and other non-Muslims.

The Bab made his pilgrimage to Mecca, but meantime hostility was arising from the establishment against his missionaries, and he himself was arrested on his return to Shiraz. The story which follows is one of continuing persecution, imprisonment, scourgings and executions. The Babis, whose creed was peace, took up arms, and defended themselves in empty military posts. For months small numbers defied the regiments of the Shah. It was a rare example of purely defensive warfare. One of the leaders, Quddus, described their strategy:

Never since our occupation of this fort have we under any circumstances attempted to direct any offensive against our opponents. Not until they unloosed their attack upon us did we arise to defend our lives. Had we cherished the ambition of waging holy war against them, had we harboured the least intention of achieving ascendancy through the power of our arms over the unbelievers, we should not until this day have remained besieged within these walls. The force of our arms would have by now, as was the case with the companions of Muhammad in days past, convulsed the nations of the earth and prepared them for the acceptance of our Message. Such is not the way, however, which we have chosen to tread. Ever since we repaired to this fort, our sole, our unalterable purpose has been the indication, by our deeds and by the readiness to shed our blood in the path of our Faith, of the exalted character of our mission. The hour is fast approaching when we shall be able to consummate the task.

Such talk is commonly propaganda or self-deceit. But this was true. The Babis would stay within their walls unless an attack was threatened, then do enough to spike the enemies' guns. They do not seem to have wanted to inflict defeat or consolidate victory. At Mazindaran and Nayriz the Babis were granted safe-conducts, and massacred by treachery; at Zanjan the fortress was eventually stormed.

The Bab himself was executed on 9 July 1850. Other followers wanted to share his martyrdom, but he said, 'Let everyone look after their own safety, for it is better that the bond of friends should continue than that all should perish.' He was shot in the presence of 10,000 watchers. It is said that the first volley, fired by Muslim troops, missed its target, and even severed the rope which held him. The Muslim soldiers thereon refused to fire again, and it was left to Christians to allow 'his holy spirit to escape from its gentle frame, and ascend to the Supreme Horizon'.

BAHA'U'LLAH

Yet the work of the Bab increased through his greater successor Baha'u'llah. Then in 1852 two young Babis in revenge for their master's death tried to assassinate the Shah. This became the occasion for massive reprisals; among those who perished was Tahirih, the one woman in the Bab's inner circle, beautiful in looks, brilliant in mind, eloquent in tongue, courageous in spirit. Baha'u'llah himself was imprisoned, but found innocent and exiled to Baghdad.

Mirza Husayn 'Ali, to give Baha'u'llah his original name, was born on 12 November 1817 in Teheran; at his birth it is said to have been prophesied that 'at this very hour the light of the Promised One has broken and is shedding illumination upon the world'. His father dreamed that the boy was swimming in the sea escorted by fishes; this was interpreted to mean that all the people of the earth would flock to him, and he would move calm and unharmed among them. As he grew up, the young man entered on the study of Islamic law, and was expected to follow other members of his family into administration. But he turned his gifts to the religious life, and it was the spiritual aspect of the law which appealed to him. It was a decisive moment when he aligned himself with the Bab, and it is said that the Bab identified him as the Promised One. During his period in Baghdad Baha'u'llah spent some time in the wilderness; it was a pattern of withdrawal and return. There followed years of teaching and writing. It was a time of danger. The hostility of those in power was mounting. He would be forced to leave for Constantinople. Before he left he retired to a garden outside the city, and there, in the last days of April 1863, pronounced to his followers that he was the Promised One, the King of Glory. The age of the Bab was over; the name Babi gave place to Baha'i.

He reached Constantinople in August and Adrianople in December. During the next five years his writing became more obviously public; he addressed his words to those in power, to Shah and Tsar, to Napoleon III and Queen Victoria and the Pope. By 1868 he was in Akko, and it was from here that the Baha'i faith spread. There was still persecution; imprisonment was to be his fortune. He met it with equanimity, giving thanks to God: 'Be glorified, O my God! Were it not for the calamities in thy love, how could the station of those who desire thee be confirmed!' Outwardly his calamity was fire and vengeance, inwardly light and mercy. He referred to himself as the Oppressed One or the Wronged One. But he showed no bitterness against his persecutors, and never sought to meet violence with violence.

THE BAHA'I FAITH

Baha'u'llah died on 29 May 1892. Leadership in the movement passed to 'Abdu'l-Baha, the Centre of the Covenant, who, in a life which lasted till 1921, spread his gospel across Europe and America. The Baha'is are people of a book. Their book consists in the authentic works of Baha'u'llah. Best known is *The Hidden Words*, a book centred upon God; union with him is heaven, separation from him is misery. Man's response is love, the cause and end of creation. His public letters to monarchs show a shrewd appraisal of the political scene combined with prophetic fervour. He is not afraid to foretell disaster, war, and revolution, and to see in them the judgement of God. One of the most important of his works is *The Most Holy Book* (*Kitab-i-Aqdas*), in which he lays down the constitutional ordinances for a new era of peace and freedom, bringing an end to class conflict and nationalist wars.

For the Baha'i faith proclaims that the new Kingdom has arrived, and that God's dominion on earth is now total and lasting. He proclaims God's victory.

The meaning of victory is not this, that anyone should fight or strive with another. . . . That which God – glorious is His mention – has desired for Himself is the hearts of His servants, which are treasures of praise and love of the Lord, and are stores of divine knowledge and wisdom. . . . Today victory neither has been, nor will be, opposition to anyone, nor strife with any person; but rather, what is well-pleasing is that the cities of men's hearts, which are under the dominion of the hosts of selfishness and desire, should be subdued by the sword of the word of wisdom and exhortation. Everyone then who desires victory must first subdue the city of his own heart with the sword of spiritual truth and of the Word, and must protect it from remembering aught but God; afterwards let him turn his efforts towards the citadel of the hearts of others. This is what is intended by victory. Sedition has never been, nor will be, pleasing to God, and that which certain ignorant persons formerly wrought was never approved by God. If you are slain for His good pleasure, verily it is better for you than that you should slay.

Cited by Townshend, *The Promise of All Ages*, p. 195.

That is unequivocal enough.

The Baha'i faith, while taking off from Islam, and deeply

influenced by Christianity, does not seek to extend any one existing religion. Rather is it an attempt to offer a single religion appropriate to a united world. It is God-centred, but there are no prescribed rites or professional clergy. It starts from the conversion and responsibility of the individual. The individual convert is called to see himself as a citizen of the world. Baha'u'llah said in conversation: 'Let not a man glory in this that he loves his country; let him rather glory in this, that he loves his kind.' He is governed by two laws, the law of justice (or Do as you would be done by) and the law of mercy (which enjoins the service of others in despite of self). The primary practical task laid on his followers by Baha'u'llah was the unification of mankind.

It might be thought that this would go no further than a vague religiosity. But Baha'u'llah's letters to those in political power have been worked over and expounded in terms related to political organization – a World Commonwealth or Super-State; an International Executive; an elected World Parliament: a Supreme Tribunal: a single International Code of Law: a World Citizenship; the abolition or limitation of national rights of taxation and armament and their transfer to the world authority; an international language; economic justice (with interdependent rights of Capital and Labour): an end to religious fanaticism and racial animosity. It is a combination of apocalyptic vision, political idealism, and practical proposals.

The Baha'is are a relatively small group with adherents numbering somewhat over a million. The administrative centre is in Haifa, and there are temples at Ishqabad in Russian Turkestan, and at Wilmette near Chicago. It is curious, in view of Baha'u'llah's approaches to political leaders that a Baha'i today is not permitted to participate in political action, contact with government, or deputations to members of Parliament. The International Baha'i Community is, however, officially recognized by the United Nations. It is interesting as a religion in which the challenge to a divided world has from the first been among its primary concerns.

FOR FURTHER READING

Balyuzi, H. M., *Baha'u'llah.* George Ronald, 1963.

Balyuzi, H. M., *Abdu'l-Baha.* George Ronald, 1971.

Balyuzi, H. M., *The Bab.* George Ronald, 1973.

Esslemont, J. E., *Baha'u'lla and the New Era,* 4th edn. Baha'i Publishing Trust, 1974.

Shoghi, Effendi, *The World Order of Baha'u'llah.* Wilmette, Ill., Baha'i, 1955.

Townshend, G., *The Promise of All Ages,* 3rd edn. George Ronald, 1972.

Chapter 11

CONCLUSION

It is not easy from this to draw any general conclusions. At one level religion is the spiritual dimension of what is; it is a dimension of war and it is a dimension of peace. In a warring society religion will be more prominently associated with war, in a peaceable society with the gifts of peace. Sometimes special deities are charged with these functions. What exists socially is accepted, not challenged.

In religions as they develop, however, there is a tendency to challenge what is with a higher vision. What is is confronted by what ought to be. Sometimes this is a reflection of social changes. But sometimes it comes from an individual or a group, who may claim divine inspiration for their new insight. This has usually taken the form of a rejection of the unthinking acceptance of war, either by circumscribing it with religious principles of justice, or by rejecting war altogether.

There is in fact a continual tension between two pulls. One is the tendency of religions to social conformity, the tendency to be different in different societies, and to change with the times. The Zoroastrianism of the military monarchs of Persia is not identical with the Zoroastrianism of the peaceable Parsis of India. The established Christianity of the nineteenth century in Britain or America seems remote from first-century Christianity in Palestine. The Buddhists of present-day China are showing some anxiety to conform with militant Communism. It is easy to be cynical about this, and to conclude that religion is really an irrelevance, an opiate with which those in political power drug the masses so as to maintain

156

that power securely. Yet a religion must be relevant to the lives of its followers, and the religious stances appropriate to an independent nation-state in Palestine may not be those appropriate to businessmen and artists scattered through the world and deprived of political power.

But if the pull were all towards social conformity cynicism might justifiably be the order of the day. It is, however, in tension with a pull in the other direction, towards criticism of the existing institutions, towards nonconformity. The founders of the great religions, such as Zarathustra, or Gautama, or Jesus, or Muhammad, have been nonconformists and revolutionaries. And all religions have thrown up from time to time those who have gone back to the vision of the founder, or sometimes gone beyond it. The Christian society which threw up the soldier Cromwell also threw up the pacifist Fox.

The result of these pulls has been paradoxical. Of the great religions Christianity and Buddhism have been the most clearly pacifist in their origins and essence. Yet both have been deeply involved with militarism from a fairly early stage in their history, and Christianity, in particular, has an appalling record of bloodshed, and has been the religion of the militant nationalisms of Europe. Taoism similarly produced the bloody uprising of the Yellow Turbans. Zoroastrianism, Islam and Shinto have been the most clearly militarist in their origins and essence. Yet Islam produced Abdul Ghaffar Khan and Shinto produced Bunjiro.

Does religion matter then? The answer in cold historical fact is that surely it does. Not just as a comfort to the consciences of large-scale kleptomaniacs and as an instrument for maintaining their power. Religions have been so used, often in the history of mankind. But we can see the pressures to social conformity and readily understand how they come about. These are the pressures of society on religion. It is the other call that is less easy to explain away, the challenge of the prophet to society to change in the name of a higher morality and an ultimate truth. This has mostly been proclaimed in the name of God or Heaven or the Way. It still comes today.

INDEX

INDEX

INDEX